Flyfishing Small Lakes for Trout

MAY ALL YOUR TROUT BE WHOPPER'S

A Guide for Beginners

by

Gordon Honey and Kenneth Strand

**Illustrations
by
Kenneth and Elna Strand**

Cover Photo by Brian Chan

Flyfishing Small Lakes for Trout: A Guide for Beginners

ISBN 0-9685128-0-1

Honey & Strand Publishing
c/o Gordon Honey
P.O. Box 5008
Lac Le Jeune, BC
V1S 1Y8
Phone: (250) 828-1286
e-mail: gordon_honey@bc.sympatico.ca

First printing September, 1999

Printed by Hignell Book Printing, Winnipeg, Manitoba

Design & Layout
Bishop & Bishop Advertising & Public Relations
Kamloops, British Columbia

Acknowledgements

I wish to acknowledge my wife, Debbie, for her unconditional support of my piscatorial career and for her companionship both on and off the water. I am indebted to so many knowledgeable fishing friends who have shared their observations and skill over the years. If I tried to name them all it would fill a book and I'm sure someone would be missed.

I must however, thank Jack Shaw and the late Hebe Smith for their teachings and kindness to a rookie years ago, Brian Chan for sharing both his scientific and fishing skills over the years and, of course, my pal and dry-fly tutor, D. K. "Buster" Ellis.

Finally to my clients (friends) who encouraged me too "put it all in a book" and to my friend and co-author Ken Strand for his making this book possible and for his scholarly work.

Gordon Honey

I wish to acknowledge the editorial and design help given by my wife, Elna. This help, plus her personal fishing tips, were major contributions to the content and completion of this book. In addition, I wish to acknowledge the contribution of three others.

The first is Dale Sullivan who introduced me, and my wife, to flyfishing and with whom we have had the privilege of fishing with over the years. We acknowledge his prowess as a practitioner of the attractor school, but his secret retrieve–the deadly "poacher's rip"–is not included in the book. To reveal it to beginners, in addition to breaking a confidence, would have the effect of stunting the development of their angling skills and endangering the fish stocks. Another is Ken Ruddick, from whom I took a course in fly tying some 25 years ago. This instruction and the fishing advice he gave were very helpful and are reflected throughout the book. The third is Brian Chan from whom I took a course on insects and lake fishing. The content of that course and his many excellent articles are also reflected throughout the book.

Kenneth Strand

Both of us wish to express our appreciation to those who read drafts of this book: Bob Brown, Tim and Elaine Burns, Brian Chan, Dale Sullivan and Wayne Yoos. Their suggestions were invaluable. The errors that remain are, of course, our responsibility.

Photos by Gordon Honey

Contents

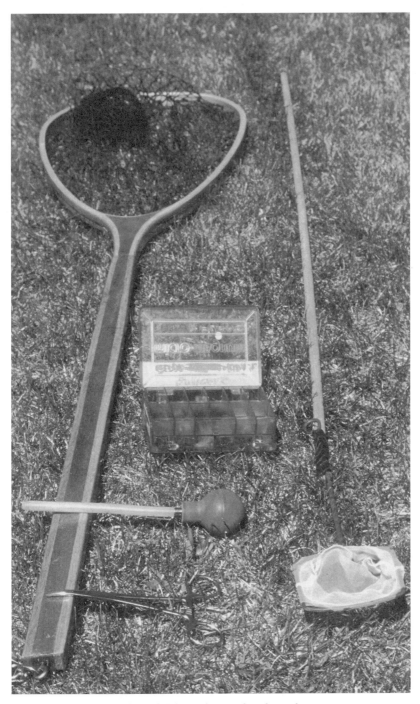

Basic Equipment for Fishing the Imitative Fly Patterns
Clockwise from lower left: landing net; forceps; stomach
pump; fly box, and an aquarium net (Chapters 3 & 6)

Chapter 1

Catching Trout on Flies

1. CATCHING TROUT ON FLIES

The Joys of Flyfishing

Flyfishing conjures the image of a fisherman on a stream enjoying a relaxing day in the wilderness. The flyline arcs gracefully and the fly settles gently on the moving water of the stream. There is a flash of silver as the fish strikes–followed by a chase through white water until the fish is landed. A sense of satisfaction combined with the beauty of the fish and the setting complete the perfect day portrayed in magazines and movies.

Flyfishing in lakes has not received the same magazine coverage that stream fishing has and its movie is yet to be made. When it is, it will feature the calm and serenity of fishing stillwater. There will be dramatic shots of the morning mist rising off the water and the sound track will carry the silence of a mountain lake broken by the haunting call of a loon. Then you will hear a high-pitched piping and your eye will be drawn skyward to a fishhawk as it glides overhead, hovers–then makes a spectacular dive into the water to catch a fish in its talons. The camera will focus on a close-up of what appears to be the limb of a dead tree. With startling swiftness, the limb of the dead tree moves and reveals itself to be a gray heron spearing a fish with its long beak for its first meal of the day. Then there will be an underwater shot and you will see a large black and white bird using its wings in a breaststroke that would be the envy of an Olympic swimmer. It is a loon in pursuit of a trout to take back to its nest to feed to its young.

When the visual joys of small lakes have been documented, the story line will shift to the trout. It will show how trout are protected from their predators by protective coloration, speed and strength. It will show the trout as a wily creature that inspects its potential foods–rejecting those that don't look right and spitting out those that don't taste right.

One of the special joys of flyfishing in lakes is that when you are not catching fish, there is always an inner voice telling you that you could catch fish if you would just "do it right". The conviction that you will outwit the wily trout as soon as you figure out how to "do it right" keeps you going as you search for the "right spot" in the lake, the "right fly" and the "right presentation". This is the challenge that holds your interest through the periods when nothing is happening.

The ultimate joy in flyfishing in lakes is when you do get it right–the moment when the line tightens, the rod bends, and your hand lifts to set the hook. You have just had your first "take" of the day. This defining moment is what makes flyfishing so different from other forms of fishing. When flyfishing in lakes, the contact between you and the fish is all touch. There is no mechanical hindrance such as a reel or a chrome flasher between you and the trout. Your hand is holding a sensitive rod and your fingers hold the thin flyline, creating a direct contact with the fly and the trout. The take is wonderfully diverse. It can be startlingly savage as a large trout attacks a leech pattern, or so subtle and deceptive that you wonder what caused you to raise your rod tip and find that a fish is, suddenly–just there. The sensation of the take can be visual as well–the gentle ring on the water surface as your mayfly pattern disappears, the heart-stopping vision of the slashing rise of a huge trout as it takes your caddis pattern. The jolt of positive energy generated by the take is why many of us fish with a fly.

Experienced anglers may be addicted to flyfishing for its solitude, its aesthetics, its mental challenge or the "rush" of the take. Unfortunately, for the beginning angler these joys seem to be hidden behind a barrier of mystical skills. This makes some reluctant to try the sport and may cause others to become frustrated and to abandon it. This need not be the case. It is our conviction that good anglers are made–not born. Simply stated, our objective is to teach you how to catch **"Walter"**–the mythical huge fish that inhabits each and every lake.

What This Book Has to Offer

If you have ever said to yourself "I wish I knew how to flyfish", this is the book for you. It is written to help people get started in the sport of flyfishing. Its focus is on fishing for trout in lakes–not in streams. It starts from the premise that the reader has no previous knowledge about flyfishing for trout in lakes and its primary goal is to enable the beginner angler to acquire the basic skills necessary to actually catch fish on a fly. Then the book shows, step by step, how these basic skills can be expanded.

This book is not just for rank beginners. If you have tried flyfishing and have become frustrated, this book is for you because it will suggest ways you might change your technique and achieve greater success.

If you already know how to catch trout in small lakes by trolling lures but have observed anglers catching fish with flies and wondered how it is done, this book is for you because it treats trolling with flies as an alternative to casting flies.

If you have lots of experience flyfishing on streams and want to apply your casting skills to lakes, this book is for you because it explains how to read a lake and how to learn the skills that are the essence of flyfishing in lakes, such as how to retrieve the fly, detect the take, and set the hook.

The book begins by asking the logical question of why flies, mere concoctions of feathers and thread, are an effective lure. The answer lies in the trout's behaviour. The trout thinks the fly is food. Accordingly the starting point for learning to catch trout is an understanding of the trout and its feeding behaviour. The beginning angler also needs simple but appropriate equipment. The array of flyfishing equipment is bewildering. Beginning anglers often buy inappropriate equipment and spend more money then necessary. After describing the function of the rod, the reel, and various lines, we recommend suitable equipment for learning to flyfish in lakes.

It is not sufficient just to understand how trout behave and to have proper equipment. The fish must be induced to take the fly and the fish must be landed. We place major emphasis on the core skills of presenting the fly, detecting the take, setting the hook and landing the fish.

Once those basic skills are understood, it is time to try them and to begin the process of perfecting them. At this point we bring knowledge of trout behaviour, proper equipment and angling skills together. We describe how to choose a lake and how to fish it–using only four all-purpose flies. Our goal is to make your first adventure into lake flyfishing a pleasant and rewarding experience.

Confident that your first experiences will encourage you to perfect your skills and expand your knowledge, we move on to slightly more advanced techniques. We recommend enlarging the fly box by adding eight imitative patterns designed for use when fish are feeding on specific foods. We explain how and when to use these proven patterns. This explanation is organized in terms of the seasonal availability of the trout's food and describes how to fish on any given day.

We also include a special section on fishing chironomid patterns. It is our observation that beginning anglers go fishing when they can (which may not be often); accordingly, a book on how to begin flyfishing ought to include techniques that work throughout the season. Chironomids are available to trout virtually all season long as it is the longest and strongest of all the hatches. Our section on chironomid fishing may be of particular interest to anglers who feel frustrated when they see others catching fish when they are not. Often those who are catching fish, when others are not, are fishing chironomids. Lack of knowledge about chironomid fishing is often regarded as the biggest obstacle to becoming a skilled angler. This section is designed to assist that transition.

After a chapter containing suggestions on ways to learn more about trout, insects, equipment and technique, the book concludes with two appendices. The first is entitled "Terms You May Hear Anglers Use". Contrary to what the title suggests, this is not a collection of curses invented by disgruntled anglers but rather the definition of some terms used in the text and other technical terms used by anglers. The second, "Knots", describes how to tie the knots we use and is at the back of the book for your convenience.

Throughout this book, we use imperial measurement units rather than metric. There are two practical reasons for this choice. Since most fishing equipment is made in the United States, it makes sense to use U.S. measurements when describing equipment. Our second reason is more personal and has to do with age.

Chapter 2

What You Need to Know

2. WHAT YOU NEED TO KNOW

Rainbow Trout

There are several types of trout but our focus is on the rainbow trout. Its natural habitat is the western United States and Canada. Rainbow trout have dark backs with silver sides and bellies. When mature, they have a characteristic reddish stripe along the side. They are avidly pursued by anglers not only for their beauty but for their fighting ability and delicious taste.

Given an abundant food supply, trout in lakes will rapidly grow to one or two pounds. An even more abundant food supply, balanced with a proper trout population, will produce five to six pound fish, or even larger. The fish that anglers will encounter most often will be in the one to two pound class. Trout live to be six or seven years old and sometimes longer, depending on the subspecies.

To reproduce, trout move out of lakes into tributary streams to lay their eggs in gravel beds. Rainbow trout spawn in the spring at three to four years of age. Spawning fish darken in colour and their flesh can become soft. Spawning activity also saps the vitality of the fish. After they spawn they return to the lake, where they quickly regain their prime condition and bright colours. Since not all of the fish in a lake will be spawning in any given year, there are prime fish available to anglers even during spawning season.

Natural spawning is often augmented by "stocking"–the introduction of hatchery fish. A well managed stocking program increases the total number of fish available by supplementing the natural increase in lakes that get heavy fishing pressure or where the natural spawning conditions are poor. Fishery management through stocking can balance trout population and food sources to provide fishing experiences ranging from lakes with an abundance of smaller fish (which are great places to learn to fish) to lakes with fewer, but larger, more challenging fish.

Trout have three specific habitat requirements that are important in understanding their behaviour. They require **food, oxygen** and **protection from predators**. The major food sources for trout are the subject of the next section.

Oxygen is the most important factor influencing trout

behaviour. Trout die without oxygen. This often happens in lakes and is called "winter kill" and "summer kill". The amount of oxygen required by a trout is directly related to the temperature of the water. For example, trout require four times as much oxygen in water at 75 degrees F. as they do in water at 40 degrees. Trout are cold blooded and since they cannot regulate their body temperatures, they will move up and down in the water column to find water temperatures most conducive to their survival. They prefer to be in water between 50 and 65 degrees F.

Trout in lakes also seek cover from their predators. Their primary predators are birds. Ospreys, also known as fishhawks, hunt fish from the air and dive into the water after their prey. The diving bird hitting the water is a spectacular sight. Fish hide from ospreys by avoiding shallow water on bright sunny days. They also seek cover in weeds or in shady areas where they are hidden from above. The loon, a beautiful black and white water bird, lives almost exclusively on a diet of fish. Loons swim underwater in pursuit of their prey; they are extremely fast swimmers and there is little fish can do to avoid them.

What Trout Eat

The 'Magnificent Seven'

The beginning angler often asks: "Why are artificial flies an effective lure?" The simple answer is that the trout thinks that the fly is food.

To become a successful angler it is therefore necessary to understand the feeding behaviour of trout and the nature of their food.

This raises the question of what trout eat.

The short answer is "bugs". This knowledge is enough to carry you a long way. In fact, in the next chapter, we suggest you start fishing with just four flies which we recommend because of their "buggy" qualities.

However, in time, it will pay you to refine your knowledge of what trout eat and you will learn that trout feed on "freshwater invertebrates". This is true, but it won't help you catch fish.

What will help you catch fish is to limit your first foray into entomology to the seven food sources that constitute the bulk of the diet of trout. These "magnificent seven"–in order of seasonal availability to trout–are:

- shrimp
- leeches
- chironomids
- dragonflies
- damselflies
- mayflies
- caddisflies

It is important to understand each of these foods. Learning to observe and identify the insect life in a lake is a basic skill essential to successful flyfishing. Knowing what they look like, and how they move through the water, will help you choose the right flies to use and the right way to present them. Knowing their habitat will help find the right place to fish. In the following section we present stylized drawings of the trout's food which are not anatomically exact but which highlight the distinguishing features that will enable you to identify them.

The Non-insects: The Shrimp and the Leech

The shrimp is a crustacean and the leech is a worm. Leeches and shrimp spend their entire lives under water and, over time, they simply grow larger. They are available to trout at all seasons of the year–which explains why they are such an important food source for trout.

Shrimp. In the early part of the season, shrimp will be in the weed-grown shallows close to the bottom. Later in the season, shrimp move to deeper water. Shrimp are oval and range in length from one-half to one inch. They look like a smaller version of the salt water shrimp that grace our salads– which is probably why they are called "shrimp" rather than the more correct name of "scuds".

Shrimp

We think of shrimp as being pink but lake shrimp take on the colour of their habitat. Accordingly, they are most often some shade of green but can be yellow, brown or gray.

Shrimp are semi-transparent and pregnant shrimp have an orange spot on their abdomen–the egg sac. Shrimp are available all year and are a staple in the trout's diet. Trout will feed on shrimp except during major insect hatches or emergences, or when warm water temperatures limit their overall feeding activity.

Shrimp swim about 6 to 12 inches at a time and then stop to rest. When stopped, they sink toward the bottom, usually in a curled position. The swimming and sinking movements are erratic–not rhythmic. Shrimp are most active at night or when light levels are low.

To find shrimp to look at, get a stick and stir up the very shallow lake bottom near the edge of a lake. See what moves. Chances are you will see shrimp. Watch them and notice how they swim. Catch one and watch it curl up.

Leeches. Leeches are found in almost all shallow lakes. They are bottom dwellers and can be found along the shoreline, especially where weed beds offer cover. It is not easy to find a big leech to look at, but look in shaded areas for a dark wormlike thing, one to two inches long. You can often find small leeches on the bottom of a boat just after it is pulled from the water.

Leech

Most leeches are mottled, spotted or striped. The common colours are black, maroon, brown, green and gray. They are available to trout year-round and are another staple in the trout's diet. Leeches are most active nocturnally but sometimes can be observed swimming in open water during daylight. They swim in an undulating up-and-down motion.

The Insects

The remaining five foods (the chironomid, dragonfly, damselfly, mayfly and caddisfly) are insects. These insects live underwater until they mature. When mature, they move to the surface, where they either hatch or emerge into their adult reproductive form. After mating, the female returns to the water to lay its eggs–which begins the cycle over again. One of the interesting things about flyfishing is that you become aware of the fascinating world which exists under the surface of the lake. It is a complex ecosystem of interdependent life that most people never notice.

Aquatic insects go through at least two and sometimes three underwater stages before becoming airborne adults. All begin as eggs which hatch into either larva or nymphs. These are the principal underwater stages for all aquatic insects. Dragonflies and damselflies become adults directly from the nymphal stage. Caddisflies and chironomids remain in the larval stage until they mature into pupa, when they rise to the surface and hatch as adults. Mayflies have a similar life cycle but have two stages after they hatch. Anglers commonly refer to insects–whether in their nymphal or pupal stages–as "nymphs".

Other than the egg stage, each stage in the life cycle of an insect constitutes a food source for trout. The nymphal and pupal stages are the most important to the trout; however, the hatches and emergences, when trout feed on or near the surface of the water, can provide the most exciting flyfishing. Unfortunately, these occur only for relatively short periods.

Chironomids. Although we call all the patterns we use "flies", the chironomid is the trout's only major food source that is a true fly in the biological sense. This insect progresses through the three cycles of larva, pupa and adult. The fully developed pupa has a long thin segmented abdomen and a large thorax, which contains the wings of the adult. White tufts are prominent at the head and to a lesser extent at the tip of the abdomen. The chironomid pupa can be as long as one inch; however, the average length is about half an inch. The most common pupa colours are black and shades of brown or green.

Chironomid Pupa

The ascent of the pupa is the most important stage for the angler as trout feed actively on the ascending pupa. Chironomid pupae do not swim to the surface; instead the movement is a slow ascent assisted by gas trapped beneath the pupal skin. Because of this gas, once the ascent begins the chironomid must rise to the surface. It cannot swim back to the bottom of the lake. During the ascent, the pupa maintains a constant undulating motion that keeps its head up and its tail down. Often it takes some time for the pupa to wriggle through the surface film. The transformation of the pupa to an adult at the surface generally takes less than two minutes. Because chironomid pupa originate from muddy bottoms, it is difficult to find one to look at until just before it reaches the water surface to hatch. When you find a hatch, use the aquarium net we recommend in the next chapter to snare one to look at.

Although the adult chironomid is not of great importance to the beginning angler, it is important to be able to identify them in order to find the pupa. Adults vary greatly in terms of size and colour. They look similar to a mosquito without the stinger. Their long thin bodies may be black, gray or light green and the wings may be dark or pale. The very small ones are smaller than a mosquito and the large "bombers" are nearly one inch long. Chironomids are very common all through warm weather. If the air is filled with insects and you aren't being bitten, they are probably adult chironomids.

Seasonally, the major chironomid hatches occur when the water warms to about 50 degrees F. and continue until about August. There is also a fall hatch in September and October. On a daily basis the hatch begins about 9 a.m.

Dragonflies. Adult dragonflies are well known and easily recognized; however, for anglers the only important stage in the life of the dragonfly is the nymphal stage. This is because trout seldom feed on the adult.

There are two types of dragonflies–the mud dweller and the weed dweller. Both live underwater as nymphs for as long as four years before emerging as adults. Both move by propelling water through the tip of the abdomen. Usually these nymphs move slowly, but they can move very quickly in short bursts.

Dragonfly Nymphs

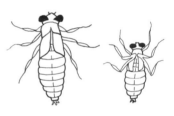

Weed Dweller   Mud Dweller

The weed dwellers average about one and a half inches in length and have oblong bodies. The most common colours are brown-black and shades of green. These nymphs are found in a wide range of lake types and are usually hidden under logs, rocks or submerged vegetation. They are active swimmers.

The mud dwellers average less than an inch in length and are short and stubby with long spider-like legs. They are lighter in coloration and can include shades of yellow, olive green and light brown. They are often found half buried in mud or well hidden in vegetation and are more sedentary than the weed dweller.

It is almost impossible to find a mud dweller to look at unless you dig around in the muddy bottom of a weed bed. Weed dweller nymphs are almost as hard to find. Very rarely will they be seen in open water and the best place to find them is to look on logs or on a dock when they have just crawled out of the water but have not yet broken out of their casing to emerge as adults.

Dragonfly nymphs are available to trout year-round and trout like them because they are large and provide a lot of food for little exertion. The nymphs are most available during their active feeding period, which is when light levels are low–at dawn, dusk or at night. However, trout feed most actively on dragonfly nymphs during their emergence. At this time, developed nymphs swim to shore and crawl up on vegetation to emerge as adults. The emergence begins in June and normally lasts from early morning to midday.

Damselflies. The adult damselfly looks like its cousin the dragonfly except it is smaller with a slender body, which is often bright blue; however, it is the nymphal stage of the damselfly that is of most importance in lake fishing. Large damselfly populations are associated with lakes having abundant vegetation. The nymphs are commonly found along the edges of the lake in water ranging in depth from a few inches to ten feet. The damselfly nymph lives underwater from six months to a year before swimming to the shore to crawl out of the water onto a reed or twig, where it emerges as an adult.

The damselfly nymph is about three-quarters of an inch long with a long thin abdomen ending in three tail-like gills. It has a large head and a prominent compound eye on each side.

It is easy to find a damselfly nymph to look at if they are emerging. You can either take one off a reed or pick one out of the water as it swims toward shore.

The mature nymph has well developed wing pads extending from the thorax.

The nymph reflects the colour of its environment. The most common colours **Damselfly Nymph** are a golden yellow or an olive green.

Damselfly nymphs are available to trout all year but the most active feeding is during the emergence, which takes place after the water warms and usually peaks about the first week in July. This migration usually takes place from mid-morning to late morning, but on cold days it may not take place until the afternoon. The nymphs swim slowly to shore. They swim close to the surface with frequent rests. The swimming motion of the damselfly nymph is very distinctive as it uses its broad tail-like gills to wiggle sideways through the water. The emergence of a damselfly is an interesting process and worth watching. The nymph slowly crawls up a reed or twig, the case splits, and the adult crawls out. As the body dries, the crystalline wings gradually unfurl and soon the beautiful adult flies away. During the process, birds often feed on the helpless insects and if you see birds feeding in the reeds, it is usually a sign of a damselfly emergence.

Mayflies. There are many species of mayflies but fortunately for the lake angler only one is of major importance– the *Callibaetis*. Like all mayflies, the *Callibaetis* has a complex life cycle. It has one underwater stage but two adult stages. The nymph hatches on the water surface into a "dun" and after it is airborne it transforms into its mature adult stage, an "imago". For anglers, the nymphs and the duns are the most important. The nymphs have a pronounced thorax and a tapered abdomen ending with three long tails. Both nymphs and adults range in length from five-sixteenths to one-half of an inch. Commonly, the nymph is a mottled olive tan and lighter on the underside. Its wing pads darken as it becomes ready to emerge.

The nymphs are found in dense vegetation on shoals no deeper than 20 feet and more often no deeper than 10 feet. When the nymph is mature and ready to emerge, it swims to the surface. This swim is aided by trapped gas in the skin and the actual emergence takes place very quickly. Newly hatched duns have a mottled dark gray body, large wings and a characteristic long upswept tail. They do not move or swim around on the surface. Instead they sail along in the wind like miniature sailboats until their wings dry and they can fly away. In the air, mayflies move in a graceful up-and-down motion. This "dance" in the air is a characteristic unique to mayflies.

Mayfly Nymph   Mayfly Dun

It is hard to find a mayfly nymph to examine because they live in dense weeds and because they hatch quickly. If you are lucky you can catch one with your aquarium net just before it hatches. The duns, on the other hand, are easy to catch. They will be all over you and your boat or tube, or you can just pick one of the little sailboats off the water. You can get a good idea of what the nymph looks like by looking at the body of the dun.

The hatch occurs between mid-May and mid-June with the

timing regulated by water temperature and daily weather patterns. The daily emergence is usually from 10 a.m. to 3 p.m. and is stronger if the sky is overcast, if there is a light breeze or if there is a light rain shower. The location of a mayfly hatch is determined by observing duns on the water, by the "bulges" as the trout takes a nymph just below the surface, or by the "splashy" rise as a trout takes a dun off the surface. This hatch can provide exciting fishing as trout often feed very aggressively on duns. Anglers, since flyfishing began, have eagerly awaited the mayfly hatch.

Caddisflies. There are two major varieties of the caddisfly– the "traveller sedge" and the smaller "cinnamon sedge". Both progress through the three stages of larva, pupa and adult. For the beginning angler, the pupa and adult stages are most important. You will hear both "sedge" and "caddisfly" used to refer to this insect. Caddis larvae live in depths of 20 feet or less amid dense growths of vegetation for up to two years, until they reach the pupal stage. A fully developed pupa ranges in length from one-quarter to three-quarters of an inch, depending on the species. It has a small head, a well-developed thorax and a long, almost bulbous abdomen, which is curved and segmented. The colour of the thorax can be brown, gray or tan with the body in shades of green or brown, some of which are segmented with yellow bands.

Caddisfly Pupa

Caddisfly Adult

When fully developed, the pupa leaves the larval case and swims to the surface at a long ascending angle. Fully emerged adults pop to the surface and will either rest there or scamper around until their wings dry.

The adult traveller sedge is a large insect (three-quarters to one inch long) with moth-like wings which it folds neatly along its back when at rest. It is a light gray-beige colour. The cinnamon sedge is smaller but a beautiful red-brown colour.

Because adult caddisflies flutter or travel around on the surface, it is easy to catch one to examine. During a hatch they often show up on your tube or boat. Caddis larvae are also easy to find. Look under rocks along the shoreline or watch for "crawling sticks" when you stir up the water looking for shrimp. Caddis pupae are more difficult to catch. Keep your eyes peeled during the hatch and maybe you can get one with your aquarium net. Seasonally, the emergence occurs from the middle of June well into July depending on elevation. Daily, the emergence is generally midday; however, some species emerge in the evening or at night. The location of a caddis hatch is determined by observing the adults scampering on the surface, birds taking insects off the surface and by the rise form. Trout take the adult caddis with a splashy rise, or even a clearing rise, coming up out of the water to come down on top of the caddis.

Generalizations

Habitat. The first and most important generalization is that all of these food sources live in the shallow portion of the lake–the "shoals"–which are up to about 20 feet deep. At these depths, sunlight penetrates enough to warm the water and allow vegetation to grow. They have the same primary needs as trout–food and protection from predators. Both of these are found in the weed beds that grow on the shoals. Note that while the trout's food is most apt to be found on the shoals, this warmer zone provides the least oxygen and cover for trout. The key to understanding the feeding behaviour of trout in a lake is to understand how they reconcile this conflict between the need for food that lives in the warm shoal water and the need for protection and oxygen provided by the deeper, cooler water.

Daily and seasonal patterns. From our description of individual insects it is clear that the emergences and the hatches have a daily pattern–they tend to begin in the morning and end in the early afternoon. This daily pattern can vary given weather conditions and an important exception is that the caddisflies sometimes hatch at night. Their seasonal pattern is summarized in the following table. (A small x denotes a minor hatch.)

SEASONAL AVAILABILITY OF FOOD SOURCES

FOODS	APR	MAY	JUN	JUL	AUG	SEP	OCT	NOV
SHRIMP	X	X	X	X	X	X	X	X
LEECHES	X	X	X	X	X	X	X	X
CHIRONOMID HATCH	X	X	X	X	x	X	X	
DRAGONFLY EMERGENCE			X	X	X	X		
DAMSELFLY EMERGENCE			X	X	x	x		
MAYFLY HATCH		X	X	x	x			
CADDISFLY HATCH			X	X				

Unique movements. The beginning angler should also be aware that each of the trout's food sources has a unique movement under the water. This is important and in Chapter 6 we discuss how to retrieve a fly so that you imitate the movement through the water of the trout's food.

- The shrimp's moves are short and erratic.
- The leech moves by an undulating up-and-down motion.
- The dragonfly nymph moves in short spurts.
- The damselfly nymph moves by wiggling from side to side.
- The mayfly nymph hatches by a slow swim to the surface.
- The caddisfly pupa hatches by a long ascending swim to the surface.
- The chironomid pupa hatches by a slow steady ascent to the surface.

Insects which hatch have a distinctive movement on the surface after they hatch. Knowing these movements will help you identify insects or imitate the actions of the insects with your fly.

- Chironomids simply pop out of their casings and fly away.
- Mayflies float on the surface until their wings dry. They are easily identified because they look like miniature sailboats.
- Caddis flies are also easily identified as they look like moths that fold their large wings flat along their bodies. They scamper or travel on the surface and make many false starts before they fly away.

Unique shapes. Each of the food sources has a unique shape. It is important that beginning anglers learn to identify the insects in their various life stages so that they can identify the specific insects on which the trout are feeding. More information on how to do this is presented throughout the book.

Feeding Behaviour

In this section, the focus shifts from the food trout eat to the factors that cause trout to feed on this food. The presence of food is, of course, a necessary condition but trout do not always feed when food is readily available. Their feeding behaviour is influenced by many factors–some of which the angler can only respond to and others, which are subject to the angler's control.

Factors You Cannot Control

Oxygen. The trout's food is most apt to be in the top layer of water–but this layer is also the warmest, which decreases the amount of oxygen in the water. Thus, when the water temperature rises, trout move to deeper, colder water with more oxygen and away from their food, which, of course, reduces their feeding. This is what leads to the "summer doldrums"–a period when trout either stop feeding or feed at depths in excess of 25 feet, where it is more difficult to present a fly.

Water temperature. When the temperature is below about 40 degrees F., trout become inactive. They are most active at about 55 degrees F. The activity of insects is also influenced by water temperature and they often hatch when water temperature is about 55 degrees F.

Barometric pressure. Both trout and their food sources are sensitive to barometric pressure. When the barometer is steady, both are active; however, when the barometer drops both trout and their food sources become less active and fishing slows down. Conversely, when the barometer rises, fishing picks up. The best fishing is when the barometer is high and steady.

Wind. Wind can be the angler's friend or worst enemy. It is a friend when it is light enough to cause a light chop or riffle. Calm water makes trout more visible to their predators and, for protection, trout move to deeper water, away from their food sources. A wind riffle reduces visibility and provides cover for the trout, so they move from deep water to feed. Wind is an enemy when it is so strong that it makes casting difficult or it roils the water. A common adage among anglers is to forget about fishing when the wind has created long white streaks of foam. Wind is also associated with weather changes and falling barometric pressure. Another common adage among anglers is if the wind is from the East–forget fishing.

Cloud cover. An overcast day induces feeding in two ways. The first is that hatches are better on overcast days. The second is that cloud cover, like a wind riffle, reduces visibility and provides cover for trout.

Rain. A light rain, like a light wind, breaks up the surface of the water and reduces visibility, providing cover for trout. Jack Shaw, a highly respected observer of lakes and fish, has pointed out another impact of a rain squall, in that when the low pressure preceding a rain squall depresses the lake, the bite is off. But, as the squall passes, the pressure is lifted and the waves and rain on the surface oxygenate the water, creating a "natural oxygen high"–and the bite is on.

Darkness. Fish often feed at night. They have excellent

night vision and at night they are protected from their predators and their food sources are active. An evening rise can be observed on most lakes and can provide excellent fishing. This night-time feeding activity is most pronounced when there is a full moon. During the period of a full moon, daytime fishing is often slow because the fish have gorged themselves feeding in the light of the moon.

Factors You Can Control

Noise. Water is an excellent conductor of sound. As a result underwater noise created by the angler spreads out and causes trout to seek cover. A major source of such noise comes from hitting the boat with a hard object such as an oar. One way to reduce such noise is to place indoor-outdoor carpet in the bottom of the boat. Unfortunately, the carpet does little to muffle loud talking.

Water disturbance. When the water surface is disturbed trout stop feeding and seek cover. Anglers disturb the water surface when they throw anchors overboard, rather than placing them gently into the water, or with sloppy casts, which lash the water. Boaters disturb the water when they use outboard motors to power into or out of a prime fishing area.

Tip

- Boaters should cut their power and either row or use an electric motor when entering or leaving a fishing area being used by others.

Visibility. Fish have excellent vision. Sudden movements and unnatural colours tend to distract them and cause them to seek cover. Avoid bright clothing, excessive false casting and standing up in the boat. Some anglers go so far as to paint their boats and oars with non-reflective black paint in order to reduce reflections.

Attitude. The best anglers have a very positive attitude. They are convinced that each cast will catch Walter and, as a result, they fish each cast with focus and intensity.

I get a kick out of my clients on their first day of fishing with a fly. When I take a small chironomid or other pattern and attach it to their leader, the response is always the same: "How can a fish find such a tiny thing in all that water and how can I possibly catch a fish on that tiny fly?" My patented response is always: "They will find it and you will catch one, but only if you have PFA." What is PFA, you ask? A Positive Fishing Attitude–don't leave home without it! – **Gord**

Brian Chan Photo

Chapter 3

Basic Equipment

3. BASIC EQUIPMENT

Flies

The most important piece of equipment is the fly. It is the interface between the angler and the fish. The rest of the equipment is designed for only one purpose–to enable the angler to present the fly to the trout.

Types of Flies

Our review of food sources has shown that trout feed both under the water and on the surface when insects are hatching. Therefore, there are two basic types of flies–wet flies and dry flies.

Wet flies. Wet flies are designed to be fished under the surface of the water. They represent leeches, shrimp or insects in their aquatic stages. Wet flies generally imitate the body parts of the food. They usually have a tail made of hair or feathers; an abdomen (the body of the fly) made of some material wrapped around the shank of the hook; a thorax, which is the thicker part behind the head (in the insect, the thorax contains the developing wings); and a head, which is usually tightly wrapped thread or a bead. There may also be some feathers to represent legs.

Dry flies. Dry flies represent adult insects after they have hatched. They have a tail and a body or abdomen, but are characterized by imitation wings made of stiff feathers or "hackle"–the feather ruff behind the head of the fly. It is the tail and the hackle that enable the dry fly to float on the surface.

You will often hear the term "hackle" when discussing flies–both wet and dry. Hackle is a feather taken from the breast or neck of a bird. Stiff hackle is used to imitate wings and to make dry flies float. On wet flies, softer hackle feathers are used and may be wrapped around the body, behind the head or used to imitate tails or legs. On leech patterns, soft hackle is used to imitate the flowing movement of the leech as the fly is pulled through the water.

Flies are tied on hooks of various sizes, lengths, shapes and weights. All of this variation is important to those who tie their own flies, but for the beginning angler, who will be buying tied flies, only the size is important. Sizes are indicated by numbers and the larger the number, the smaller the hook.

Flies Trout Prefer

You will have noticed a large selection of flies in your fly shop. Some are rather sombre in colour and closely resemble insects. Others are brightly coloured and look like no known insect. There are two theories as to which flies trout prefer. The "matching" theory holds that the effectiveness of a fly and its presentation is determined by the accuracy with which the fly imitates the food that fish eat. The "attraction" theory holds that it is the inherent abstract attractiveness of the fly, and its presentation, which triggers the strike. While "matching" vs. "attraction" leads to spirited debate among experienced anglers, it is our observation that it is a source of confusion for beginners. We note that there are expert anglers in each camp and the important thing is what works. On balance, we are closer to the matching school in that we think that shape, size and colour, in that order, are the important things to match. In other words, the fly need not be–and often should not be–a perfect imitation of the food source.

The Minimal Fly Box

Our experience has shown that beginning anglers are best served by starting with attractor patterns and then moving to more imitative "matching" patterns as their skill levels increase. We suggest that as a beginner, you start with a "minimal" fly box. This fly box consists of the following four "attractor" patterns, each in a single size. These flies are for all-purpose use and are not intended to match specific insects. What they have in common is that they look "buggy". These flies are generally available in fly shops and are pictured in colour in the centre of this book.

		SIZE
Wet flies	Black Doc Spratley with a silver rib	10
	Olive Woolly Bugger	8
	Halfback	10
Dry fly	Humpy with a black body	10

The **Doc Spratley** is an excellent fly to use when exploring a lake. To the fish it may represent leeches, chironomids, caddis pupa, damselfly nymphs, mayfly nymphs or immature dragonfly nymphs.

The **Woolly Bugger** is another good fly for exploring a lake. In its purest form, it represents a leech; however, one can increase its versatility by "clipping and ripping". If a Woolly Bugger is altered by clipping the hackle off the back half of the fly and by ripping off most of the tail section, it will resemble a dragonfly nymph. Alternatively, if one clips off all of the hackle except for a small amount at the head of the fly, it will resemble a damselfly nymph. Finally, if one clips off all of the tail and all of the hackle from the top and along the sides, leaving only the hackle on the underside, it will resemble a shrimp.

Tip

- Don't be shy about altering flies if you think they are too fully dressed or the wrong shape. Experiment by altering the tail and hackle of a Woolly Bugger or by cutting off the wing of a Doc Spratley (see the colour photos of a clipped Woolly Bugger and a clipped Doc Spratley).

The **Halfback** is also a versatile fly. It seems to capture the essence of many insects because of its clearly defined tail, abdomen and thorax. To the fish, this fly may represent chironomid pupae, damselfly nymphs, mayfly nymphs, caddis pupae or shrimp.

The **Humpy**, our dry fly pattern, is a durable, buoyant fly which does not resemble any particular insect but which trout will take during hatches and even when there is no hatch.

If any of these flies are not available, ask your local fly shop to recommend a substitute. You could also ask this question: "If you were limited to one dry fly and one wet fly, what would they be?" Buy whatever the answer is and substitute your purchase for whatever is unavailable.

Tips

- Buy two or three of each of these patterns so that you will have spares when you lose a fly in the weeds or break off on Walter.
- Don't try to save money by buying flies at your supermarket. Buy flies at a fly shop. These flies may cost a bit more but they will last longer and are more apt to catch fish.

In Chapter 6 we recommend expanding the fly box to include imitative patterns–but, at first, stick to these four flies. Given the wide variety of eye-catching flies available, it is easy to over-invest in flies. Do not be tempted to buy a fly because you like its looks. You want flies that attract trout–not flies that attract fishermen.

Each of us has been approached by beginning anglers and asked to recommend a fly from their fly box. Typically, all of the flies are too gaudy and inappropriate. Rather than recommend an inappropriate fly, we give them one or more of the attractor patterns we have recommended to you.

Rods, Reels and Lines

A beginning angler has two choices regarding the purchase of rods, reels and lines. The first is to buy a complete "beginner's kit" from a manufacturer. The second is to buy individual components and assemble one's own kit.

Beginner's Kits

Manufacturers' kits have advantages. They are complete–rod, reel and line–and they are "balanced", which means that the components have a proper relationship one to another. Another advantage is cost–these kits are relatively inexpensive. One disadvantage is that the kits are designed for beginning stream fishing and therefore include a floating line, which is the best line for learning to fish streams, but not necessarily the best way to begin lake fishing. In lakes you might want to begin by trolling a sinking line. It should be noted, however, that a floating line is the best line for learning to cast. It should also be noted that if spare spools for the reel in the kit are available, you could buy an appropriate sinking line and a spare spool to put it on. A disadvantage of these "packages" is that the rods tend to be very "soft"–which means that they have a very slow action and can be difficult for a beginner to cast.

Recommendation. The manufacturers who make these kits are those who also make the quality components available in fly shops. However, we can't recommend a specific kit because we've not had an opportunity to test them all. If cost is a primary concern, or if you are unsure as to how committed you are to learning to flyfish lakes and want to "test the water", then you should give serious consideration to buying a complete kit. However, if cost is not a primary concern we suggest working with your fly shop to develop a package of your own design which includes a rod that is stiffer than those in manufacturers' kits.

The rest of this chapter explains the function of the various components and recommends appropriate equipment for learning to fish lakes. These recommendations can be used either to evaluate complete kits or to purchase individual components.

Rods

The rod is used to provide the spring that propels the line when casting. It acts as a shock absorber when a fish strikes and when one is playing a fish it also serves as a lever to help land the fish. At one time rods were made only from split bamboo. Then fibreglass rods were developed and now almost all rods are made from graphite–which is light and strong. Go with the graphite.

Rods are designed for casting and come with different flex patterns and in different lengths. The flex patterns range from "soft" or "slow" to "stiff" or "fast". The major difference is in the butt section, with fast rods having a stiffer butt section than slow rods. Trout rods range in length from "short" (7.5 feet) to "long" (10 feet). The shorter rods are designed for use on small streams where long casts are not needed or not possible.

The distance a rod can cast a line depends on the weight of the line and "line speed"–how fast the tip of the rod moves as it propels the line through the air. Stiff rods cast a line farther than soft rods because stiff rods straighten out faster than soft rods. It is difficult to learn to cast with stiff rods because their quicker action requires more precise timing. Long rods cast a line farther than short rods. This is because for any given degree of rotation at the butt of the rod, the tip of a longer rod moves farther than the tip of a short rod and therefore must move faster.

Given all this, what is the appropriate rod for learning to fish lakes? It is our view that the rod should be relatively long– 9 feet–with a "moderate" action. In other words, it should be in between the extremes of "slow" and "fast".

The remaining question is the size of the rod. Rods are designed to match specific line weights with the stronger rods having higher numbers.

For example, a number 6 rod matches a number 6 line and is stronger and heavier than a number 5 rod. The rod should be strong enough to land a fish quickly but light enough that it is easy to cast.

Appropriate rod size is determined by the size of fish for which the angler will be fishing.

Recommendation. Since most lake fishing is for one to two-pound trout we recommend a number 6 graphite introductory rod that is 9 to 9.5 feet long, has a moderate action and is made by a major rod maker. A rod this size will handle larger fish, so don't be afraid that the rod will break when you hook Walter.

Rods also vary in terms of the number of sections, with the most common being a two-piece rod. Rods with more sections (three to five) are called "travel rods" as they are easier to transport than two-piece rods. Some manufactures make a full line of travel rods well suited to the beginner both in terms of price and action.

Tip

- Don't call your rod a "pole". Only Huck Finn and Tom Sawyer use fishing poles.

Reels

In some types of fishing, the reel is the primary tool for landing a fish; however, it has a simpler use in lake flyfishing where it is primarily used to store the line. This means that quality reels for a beginning angler can be found in the lower price range.

On most flyfishing reels the spool turns once for each turn of the handle; however, there is also the "multiplier" reel, which has gears so that the turn of the spool is some multiple of each turn of the handle. Obviously, reeling in is faster with a multiplier. This is nice and more costly but not necessary for lake fishing.

Flyfishing reels also vary in terms of size, which is matched to line size, and in terms of the "drag"–a mechanism that prevents the reel from free spooling, which causes snarls in the line.

In our view a reel should have an adjustable drag to control the resistance when the line is coming off the reel.

Recommendation. We recommend a standard-type fly reel in a size that will take a number 6 line plus 100 to 150 yards of 20-pound backing. Ask your fly shop to show you reels in this size. The reel should have adjustable drags and an exposed rim to permit you to increase the drag by pressing the exposed rim against your palm or clothing. The reel should be easily convertible from right to left-hand retrieve. Finally, separate spools should be available. The reason for this is that if you buy more lines, you need only to buy the cheaper spools rather than additional reels. Cassette-style reels are also available. They have a removable plastic cassette rather than the spool of a conventional reel.

Lines

The line has three components–the backing, the line itself and the leader.

Backing. The backing goes on the reel first and it has two functions–to fill up the spool so that each revolution brings in more fly line and to act as a "reserve" for those happy moments when Walter takes out all your line. As noted above, we recommend, depending on reel size, 100 to 150 yards of 20-pound backing.

Lines. In the days of bamboo rods the fly lines were made of silk. These lines were difficult to care for and difficult to cast. There has been a tremendous change in fishing equipment with the introduction of more modern materials–nowhere is this more evident than in lines. The use of plastics has allowed the creation of a wide array of lines with different characteristics, but they can all be divided into two broad categories: sinking lines, which are designed to be fished **under** the water surface; and floating lines, which are designed to be fished **on** the water surface.

The size or weight of a line is designated by a number–the higher the number, the heavier the line. It is important that the weight of the line balances with the strength of the rod. Casting is difficult or impossible if these two components are not well balanced.

Another distinction is whether the line is "double tapered" or "weight forward". This refers to the taper in the front portion of the line.

A weight forward line has a bulge in the front portion which creates a weight that makes the line easier to cast. The word "taper" in double tapered means the line has a smooth, progressive taper that makes for more gentle presentations and thus is more useful on floating lines in streams. The word "double" in double tapered means the line is tapered at both ends so that when the first end is worn out, the line can be reversed.

Line manufacturers use a standardized system of designation; for example WF-6-F and DT-6-F.

The first set of letters indicates whether the line is weight forward (WF) or double tapered (DT). The number indicates the line size and the final letter indicates whether the line is a floating line (F), an intermediate line (I), a full sinking line (S) or a floating line with sinking tip (F/S).

Thus, the example WF-6-F designates a weight forward size 6 floating line.

Sinking lines are now available in various densities, which control the rate at which they sink. The table below shows the various types of sinking lines and the respective sink rates expressed in inches per second.

SINKING LINES

Type of Sinking Line	Sink Rate (inches per second)
Intermediate	1.15 to 1.5
Type I	1.5 to 2.25
Type II	1.75 to 2.75
Type III	2.5 to 3.5
Type IV	4.0 to 5.0
Type V	4.5 to 6.0

Information as to the type of sinking line and the sink rate is printed on the box the line comes in. This information is separate from the weight and size designation.

Tip

- For ease in judging the sink rate of your lines, convert from inches-per-second to feet-per-minute and write this rate on the side of your boat or tube.

Recommendations. We recommend:

- Weight forward lines over double tapered lines because they are easier to cast.
- We have recommended a size 6 rod; accordingly, we recommend that you buy number 6 lines. Note, however, that many anglers increase the line size by one. They use a number 7 line on a number 6 rod, on the grounds that some rods cast better when "over-lined". Consult your fly shop.
- If, after you have read the chapter on basic skills, you plan only to troll, your first line should be a Type II sinking line. If, at some later date, you want a second line it should be a Type III line.
- If you plan only to cast, your first line should be a floating line (WF-6-F). If, at some later date, you want a second line, it should be an Intermediate sinking line (WF-6-I).
- If you plan to do both, blend the recommendations for lines.
- Buy one reel and buy spare spools for your other lines. At some point in time you might want to buy a second reel and a second rod.

Leaders. The function of the tapered monofilament leader is to provide a transition from the relatively thick fly line to the fly so that the presentation of the fly can be as unobtrusive as possible. A tapered monofilament leader has three parts:

- A butt section which is relatively heavy and attaches to the fly line
- A tapered middle section which ends in:
- A thin tippet section to which the fly is attached.

Leader packages contain the following information: length (measured in feet); breaking strength (measured in pounds); and the diameter of both the butt and the tippet (measured in thousands of an inch).

Diameter and **strength**, while related, are often confused. Diameter determines how the leader rolls out to present a fly. Larger flies require a larger diameter tippet to get them to roll over and present the fly properly.

It is for this reason that leader packages provide information on tippet diameter. What leads to confusion is that tippet diameters are designated in terms of Xs.

The following table shows the relationship between Xs and tippet diameter. This relationship is standard among manufacturers: however, the strength of any tippet size varies from manufacturer to manufacturer. Accordingly, the strengths shown are representative.

TIPPET SIZES and STRENGTHS

SIZE	DIAMETER (inches)	STRENGTH (pounds)
0X	.011	13.0
1X	.010	11.0
2X	.009	9.0
3X	.008	6.5
4X	.007	5.5
5X	.006	4.4
6X	.005	3.2
7X	.004	2.4

Note that some leader manufacturers include information as to appropriate fly sizes for each tippet diameter. This is relevant for the proper presentation of dry flies–especially on streams. Since lake fishing is predominantly with wet flies, the recommended fly sizes are largely irrelevant, and for that reason are not presented. The tippet size we recommend is appropriate for the dry flies we recommend.

Through changing flies the tippet portion of your leader will gradually get shorter. Since it is important for the presentation of the fly that the thinner tippet portion of the leader remain fairly long you can buy separate spools of tippet material in various sizes to tie on to your leader. This allows you to change the size of the tippet, if that is necessary, and to maintain a proper leader length.

Recommendations. We recommend:

• That beginning anglers buy 9 foot 4X leaders plus a spool of 4X tippet material. This leader is appropriate for the flies we recommend. When not appropriate, the leader can be modified either by cutting it back or by adding a length of tippet material.

Other Equipment We Recommend

- **A landing net.** The net should be at least 15 inches long (excluding the handle) and have a soft net, preferably cotton, as cotton is less injurious to fish than other materials. If it is to be used in boats, the net should have a long handle. It is convenient to have a net that floats, especially if you are fishing from a tube.
- **A fingernail clipper.** This is all you needs to trim leaders and tippets. If it is necessary to clean out the eye of a hook, use the point of another hook.
- **Forceps.** Forceps are very useful when removing a fly from the mouth of a fish. Smooth jawed forceps are less injurious to the fly than those with serrated jaws; however, serrated jaws can be made smooth by grinding or filing.
- **An aquarium net.** This small net, taped to a dowel, is useful to dip insects out of the water for closer observation.
- **Floatant.** Dry flies require floatant to keep them buoyant. For the Humpy in your minimal fly box, use a paste floatant. On more delicate flies a spray floatant is better.
- **Polaroid sunglasses.** These will not only protect your eyes from the sun and errant fish hooks, but will also enable you to see better into the water to spot fish and insects.
- **A plastic tool box.** You need something in which to keep your fly fishing equipment. Vests are designed for stream fishing. Baitboxes are designed for bait fishing. A simple plastic toolbox is excellent for lake fishing from a boat. If you use a tube, store your equipment in the pockets of the tube.
- **A pair of small scissors.** These are useful when you wish to trim flies.
- **A fly box.** We recommend a small compartmental box rather than one designed to hold flies by their hooks.

How to Put It All Together

Decide on Your Reel Set-up

The first decision you must make is whether to wind in the line with your right hand or your left hand. Reels come set up for a right-hand retrieve and for many this is satisfactory. It does require that one shift the rod from the right hand to the left hand if one wants to play a large fish off the reel. Many right-handed anglers prefer to do this because their right hand is more coordinated and they can reel in faster with their right hand. Reeling in the line with the left hand has the advantage that all rod work is done with the right hand and all line work is done with the left hand. Do what is most natural. If, as recommended, your reel can be easily converted from right to left-hand retrieve, you can always change.

How to Put the Line Components Together

If you bought your reel and line components at a fly shop, they will probably assemble the components for you without charge. Don't hesitate to ask. Watch them do it so you can learn how it is done. What follows assumes that you are assembling the components yourself.

Knots. The line components are tied together with knots. We use four knots–the Duncan Loop, the Nail Knot, the Perfection Loop, and the Surgeon's Knot. The following pages illustrate how these knots are used. Detailed instructions on how to tie these knots are presented in Appendix B.

Backing to the reel. The first step is to tie the backing onto the arbor of the reel. Use a Duncan Loop. Once the backing is tied on, wind it onto the reel in accordance with your decision regarding the use of the right or left hand.

Line to backing. When you open the box containing the line you will notice that on a weight forward line there will be a tag telling you which end is to be attached to the reel or backing. If you bought a double taper you can tie on either end. For this connection use a Nail Knot.

Backing   Line

Leader to line. When you open a leader package uncoil the leader by unwinding the thicker, butt end. Then stretch the leader by pulling it through your hands. The leader should be straight and fairly limp. A leader with coils or kinks in it will cause you to lose fish when they take your fly. Leaders come from the manufacturer two ways–with or without a pre-tied loop in the butt end. The same is true for lines in that some, but not all, come with a pre-formed loop in the tip of the line where the leader is to be attached.

If your line and your leader both have loops, connect them "loop to loop":

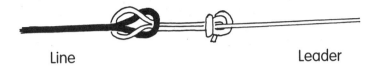

Line   Leader

If your line has a loop but your leader does not, tie a Perfection Loop in your leader and connect the leader and line "loop to loop" as illustrated above.

If neither your line nor your leader has a pre-formed loop, tie them together with a Nail Knot:

Line   Leader

If you tie your leader to your line with a Nail Knot, at a later date when your leader becomes too short for proper presentation of a fly, you can cut the leader about 10 inches ahead of the Nail knot and tie a Perfection Loop in the 10-inch section. You can now attach your new leader to your line loop-to-loop.

Line   Connector   Leader

Tippet to leader. When you have used up about 12 inches of your leader because of changing flies, you should add at least 12 inches of tippet material. The knot to use when adding tippet material is the Surgeon's Knot.

Fly to tippet. We use and recommend the Duncan Loop. Many anglers use the clinch knot to tie on a fly. It is an easy knot to tie but unless it is tied correctly, it can unravel. For this reason many anglers use the improved clinch knot. One reason we prefer the Duncan Loop is because it almost never unravels. Further, because it is a slip knot, it need not be pulled tight but can be left a bit loose so that the fly has a more natural movement. Finally, when tying on a small dry fly, the knot can be completed away from the hackle and then pulled tight without catching the hackle. It is worth taking the time to learn how to tie the Duncan Loop. It has many uses.

Rod Assembly

Assembly of the rod is straightforward; however, these tips may be useful:

- When fitting the ferrules, push them together so one section is 45 degrees off alignment and then twist them together so they are snug and in alignment.
- If the ferrules become stuck and you cannot get the sections apart, get someone to help and each of you hold one section and pull. If you immerse in cool water the section that fits inside, it will contract and allow the sections to part more easily.
- If you want to lubricate the ferrule, rub the end along the side of your nose to coat it with the oil from your skin.
- If the ferrule is too loose, rub bee's wax on the end.
- When threading the line through the guides, do not put the leader tippet end through the guides as if you were threading a needle. Instead, make a loop in the fly line and thread this loop through the guides. This makes threading easier and because it is more visible you are less likely to miss a guide. This method will also assist you if you are distracted half way through the process because the leader and line will catch in the guides and not completely fall out of the guides as the leader alone often does.

One time an expert fisherman offered to take me out on a lake and show me the hot spots. I eagerly threaded my line on my rod and announced that I was ready to go. He looked at my rod and noticed that in my eagerness I had threaded my line through the hook keeper. He tactfully pointed out that most of the fishermen he knew didn't do it that way. I was too embarrassed to make any reply.

After you have threaded your line on your rod, pull the entire leader through the guide on the tip, clamp the line tight to the handle with one hand and pull on the leader with the other. This will cause the rod to bend and you can look at the rod to make sure that the line has gone through all the guides–and only the guides.
– Ken

Tube or Boat?

It is only under exceptional circumstances that an angler can fish a lake from the bank or by wading. One must use either a boat or a float tube. This section discusses the characteristics of each and suggests how to decide between a boat or a tube.

Types of Tubes

In the early '70s I bought one of the first tubes on the market. It was a simple canvas doughnut designed to hold a truck tube. It seemed the perfect solution to fishing my favourite walk-in lake. When I asked the salesman how it was to be propelled he glibly told me to get two ping pong paddles, drill holes in the handles so that I could tie on a string and thread the string through my sleeves like school boys have strings on their mittens. Having done all this, I went out on the lake holding the rod in my teeth because there were no straps or anything to hold it. I would ping pong paddle like mad but, as you can imagine, progress was slow. I even caught a few fish in this wonderful contraption but the hilarious laughter from the shore caused me to abandon the paddles. Eventually I got flippers. – Ken

Tubes now come in various shapes–doughnuts, U-boats (these are U-shaped and not something German that goes under the water) and pontoons.

What they have in common is that they are inflatable and are propelled by kicking with flippers worn on the feet. They vary in terms of cost, ease of entry, ease of transportation and optional features.

The least expensive tube is the doughnut, closely followed by the U-boat.

The pontoon type has the broadest range of prices and can be the most expensive, depending upon the size and the options such as oars, a mount for an electric motor and provision for a cooler box.

Entry into the doughnut is most difficult. You can get into the tube by either stepping into the centre of the tube with flippers on or by putting it on over your head. In either case, you have to put your flippers on first as they are difficult to put on after you are in the tube. Then you must enter the water by walking backwards to avoid stubbing your flippers. This can be awkward if the shoreline is rough. The U-boat and the pontoon types are much easier to enter as you put them in the water and then enter through the open part between the pontoons.

Doughnuts and U-boats are the easiest to transport to a lake as they can be left inflated and carried inside a vehicle or on top. They are also the easiest to carry into a walk-in lake as they are the smallest and lightest.

It may be necessary, because of its size, to transport the pontoon type deflated. Further, dependent upon the specific design, it may be difficult to carry the larger pontoon types into a walk-in lake. As a general rule, the larger pontoon types, which are designed for use in rivers, are over-designed for use in lakes.

Whichever type you choose, insure that your tube is properly inflated. At a minimum the exterior cover should have no wrinkles. On the other hand, do not over-inflate your tube as it may explode at high altitudes.

> *A classic case happened to a friend of ours. He inflated his float tube at his home which is near sea level. As he drove over a mountain pass on the way to his favourite lake he heard a huge roar from the back of his truck. His float tube had exploded. All that was left was a tattered cover, which his wife finally sold at a garage sale.*

Advantages of Tubes

The major advantages of tubes, compared to boats, are:
- They are cheaper–even though one must also buy waders to keep dry and flippers to propel the tube.
- They are easier to transport.
- They are less intrusive–it is easier to sneak up on fish in a tube than in a boat and, as a result, shorter casts are permitted.
- Because you are closer to the water surface, tubes permit closer observation of what is happening in the immediate area.

Disadvantages of Tubes

The major disadvantages of tubes, compared to boats, are:
- Because you propel yourself backwards by kicking your feet, it is difficult to see where you are going or what is coming toward you.

- Because you are closer to the water, it is difficult to see what is happening elsewhere on the lake and it is difficult to make longer casts.
- They are slower to move around the lake because there is a limit on how fast you can move by kicking with flippers. This is important if you want to move against the wind and limits their use on large lakes.
- They limit the amount of equipment you can carry.
- There is a problem of "captivity"–one is handicapped by the waders and the slowness of movement. This can be acute if the wind comes up or if one is cursed with a small bladder or leg cramps.

Tip

- Do not buy a tube that can be inflated by mouth–they are too fragile and have been known to collapse out on the lake.

---

*I remember an incident that is now very funny but could have been tragic. Three couples had been staying at the lodge and in my comings and goings we had exchanged greetings. One afternoon they were at the boat dock teasing one of the group who was about to take his float tube on its first voyage. Calling it a float tube would be generous as it happened to be one of those mouth-inflated beauties from a big box store. As I passed the group I made a smart-assed comment like "you're really not going out in that thing are you?" and proceeded on my way. Upon returning a bit later I found the group no longer laughing but busy pulling their somewhat wet and frightened friend from the lake. The crotch strap on his mouth-inflated device had collapsed, dumping the no longer proud owner directly into the depths as if shot from a torpedo tube. Had his friends not been close at hand–who knows! DO NOT purchase a mouth-inflated float tube, please. – **Gord***

Tips

- Buy a tube that is highly visible to boaters. Remember that you are low in the water and hard to see and that because you move backwards, it is hard for you to see oncoming boaters.
- Use a two-pound downrigger ball as an anchor.

The first time you get into a float tube you will have to learn how to propel it. On your first day take everything slowly; don't attempt any world records for the 100-yard backward kick. In a tube let your legs and feet hang down in a relaxed position and kick slowly almost as if peddling a bicycle. In a pontoon boat the best technique seems to be a gentle butterfly kick.

Practice turning before you even wet a line. Turning is very easy if you don't fight it, play around with the flipper technique that suits you. For example, if you want to turn right–in either a tube or in a pontoon boat–move your right leg slightly to the right and make long slow sweeps with your right flipper.

Many of my clients have never been in a tube or pontoon boat before and will typically wear themselves out before noon without a little coaching.

Tubes can be great fun if you don't wear yourself out by thrashing about too much. The resulting cramps are a painful reminder to slow down!

If you relax and enjoy it they are very comfortable, so much so that I remember one chap who was so comfortable that he fell sound asleep and drifted about the lake for an hour as I kept my eye on him until a substantial trout rudely woke him up by almost ripping the rod from his sleepy hands.

– Gord

Types of Boats

Fishing boats are of two types–the conventional boat with a pointed prow and a rounded bottom and a pram with a squared prow and a flat bottom. Briefly stated, prams are better to cast from but the conventional boat is better for movement around a lake.

Advantages of Boats

The major advantages of boats, compared to tubes, are:
- Boats permit greater visibility of what is happening elsewhere on the lake.
- You can quickly move around the lake to areas where you see hatches or fish.
- You can stand up in a boat–to stretch or to spot fish and insects.
- Boats can hold more than one person.
- You can carry more equipment in a boat.
- Because one is higher above the water and can stand up, one can cast further from a boat and it is easier to play fish.

Disadvantages of Boats

The major disadvantages of a boat, compared to a tube, are:
- Boats are more costly. In addition to the boat, one must buy anchors, anchor lines and oars. One can rely on oars for movement or one can buy a motor–either a gasoline motor or an electric motor and a deep cycle battery.
- Boats are more difficult to transport. They have to be transported on the top of a car, in the bed of a pickup or on a boat trailer. Heavier boats can be hard to handle if you are alone. Note that aluminum boats are lighter than fibreglass boats and are more durable.
- Because of how they are propelled and because they are higher above the water boats are more intrusive and more visible to the fish and are noisier.

Recommendations. All in all, you fish more effectively from a boat than from a tube because you can observe more and you have greater mobility. However, if you do not already have a boat, rent or borrow a boat and a tube and try them out and form your own opinions.

- If you intend to fish small lakes, consider a pram and oars or an electric motor.
- If you buy an electric motor, get the largest one your budget

permits and preferably one with an infinitely variable speed control–not just a limited number of settings.

- If you intend to fish large lakes, consider a conventional boat and a gasoline motor.
- If you buy a conventional boat, consider a minimum length of 12 feet.
- If you buy a boat, be sure it has built-in floatation.
- If you intend to fish walk-in lakes, buy a tube.
- If you buy a tube, buy the best your budget will permit both for safety and longevity.
- If you buy a pram, buy the longest pram your budget will permit and the one with the highest sides–especially if you intend to have more than one person in the boat.
- Used boats are often a good buy; however, used motors should be checked very carefully.

┌─ **Tips** ─────────────────────────────────

- Do not neglect safety. Use a personal floatation device (PFD) whether in a tube or a boat. You can now buy fishing vests that are inflatable and double as life jackets. There are also inflatable harnesses designed for use with float tubes.
- If you buy a boat, cut pieces of indoor-outdoor carpet to cover the floor of the boat. The carpet will reduce noise and will also cushion the line when you step on it. Further, you can remove the pieces of carpet to shake out dirt and gravel that will damage your fly line.
- Wear only soft-soled shoes. Boots with hard soles such as hiking boots will damage your fly lines.
- Check the regulations. On some lakes, only electric motors are allowed. On others, large outboard motors may be prohibited.
- If you buy a boat, buy two anchors and about 50 feet of line for each anchor. Two anchors will keep your boat from swinging around in the wind and disturbing your retrieve. Fifty feet of line will be ample in all reasonable fishing spots.

Boat fishing does require one major factor that I see disregarded time and time again–good housekeeping! By this I mean neat and tidy with no gear bags or anchor ropes etc. in the area you are casting from. When you strip line from your reel to cast you want nothing in the area that the line can catch on. There is nothing more frustrating than attempting a perfect cast to feeding fish only to have your line catch on the anchor rope or whatever else it can find in the bottom of your boat. The resultant cast is not only short but it also scares the living daylights out of the fish.

Another classic result of an untidy boat is when after a long day with little or no success you finally hook Walter–who explodes in a huge showy jump and then takes off for the middle of the lake at the speed of light. The line peels from where it is coiled at your feet and then at the last moment catches on a buckle of your gear bag. PING! Walter swims away at his leisure with your broken leader and your treasured fly stuck firmly in the corner of his jaw. Keep your boat neat and tidy.
– Gord

Caring for Your Equipment

Your fishing equipment is valuable. The better it is maintained the longer it will last and the better it will perform.

Flies

Allow your flies to dry before putting them away. If they are put away wet, the hooks are apt to rust and become dull.

If your dry flies become matted or flat on one side they can sometimes be revived by steaming them for a few minutes in a vegetable steamer.

Rods

A rod is your most expensive piece of equipment and deserves the most care.

Use the **LIFO** method. Your rod should be the **Last In** your boat or tube and the **First Out**.

When you take it out, the most dangerous place you can put it is on top of your vehicle. Each of us have damaged rods by placing them on top of our vehicles and then driving off. Further, every year we hear of rods that were lost when the owners drove off with their rods on top of their vehicles. Put them in containers and put them away.

Reels

Once a year, remove the spool and clean the inside surface area using a Q-Tip dipped in reel oil. The Q-Tip will enable you to remove any debris from around the drag system, be it a disc or a simple click and pawl. Grease the spindle and you are done! If you get dirt or sand in your reel, clean it right away.

Lines

Clean lines are critical to good casting. You will be surprised at how dirty they are once you give them more than a cursory glance. If you have been fishing in lakes with an algae bloom, they are probably stained and will not feel smooth. Here are two simple ways to clean lines:

- Peel all the line from the reel into a bucket of warm water with dish soap in it. Swirl gently, much like the action of a washing machine. Reel the line back on to the spool through a clean cloth moistened with commercial line cleaner or reconditioner.
- Again, peel the line from your reel, but pass it through a chamois which has been soaked in dish soap. Then, as above, treat it with cleaner or reconditioner as you reel it back on the spool.

You can also keep a piece of towelling in your kit and at the end of the day's fishing, reel your lines back on the reel through the cloth.

If there are curls or kinks in your line, stretch it. The best way to stretch it is to catch Walter. If that fails, a good way is to have a friend hold the end of the line and run out about 60 feet from the reel. You then hold the reel so the spool won't turn and each of you pull. The line will stretch two to three feet and be straighter. Alternatively, you can stretch your line between two trees. When it is stretched is a good time to clean it.

Leaders

Periodically check to see if there are any curls in your leader, if so, stretch it between your hands. If this does not work, replace your leader. Also replace your leader if you have clipped off too much without replacing the tippet.

*As a fishing guide, the most common equipment error I
see is that new fly anglers do not pay enough attention
to their leaders. All too often when I check a client's
gear or that of a frustrated angler who hails me when
I'm out fishing on my own, I find a leader that is too
short. It usually ends in a stump of about 12-pound test,
making it almost impossible to tie on a fly and, if they
do manage to attach that heavy leader to a fly, no self-
respecting trout would give it a second look.*

*Some may have realized the leader is too short and
have added a length of 4X tippet material to the heavy
12-pound leader. This does indeed lengthen the leader
but the large differences in diameter weaken the leader
and cause "hinging" which in turn, ties knots in the
leader which also weaken it. Such knots are called
"wind knots" but are really caused by casting errors.*

*Others may have proper leader length but have failed
to check on a regular basis during the angling day for
wind knots and when they finally do hook Walter, their
leader will break at the wind knot–and off swims Walter
with their favourite fly.* **– Gord**

Chapter 4

Basic Skills

4. BASIC SKILLS

You now have your flies and your rod and line are assembled. It is time to learn how you are going to use your equipment to present your fly to the trout. Conditions in lakes are totally different from conditions that occur in streams. In streams, the water is moving and the fish wait for the stream to bring food to them. Presentation in stream fishing is how to cast the fly given the pattern of currents in the stream. In lakes, the reverse is true. The water is stationary and the fish move in search of food. Presentation in lake fishing is how to move the fly through the stationary water. There are two general techniques–trolling and casting.

Trolling

Trolling consists of letting line out behind a boat or tube and dragging it through the water by moving the boat or tube.

Advantages of Trolling

For the beginning angler, the major advantage of trolling is that you do not have to learn to cast so it is a good way to begin. At the same time it is an effective technique in its own right. It is particularly useful when learning a new lake or for searching for fish when there is no obvious hatch.

When you troll from a float tube the feet are used to propel the tube and, as a result, the rod is always in your hands. This is advantageous because you can feel the fish take the fly and because you can retrieve the fly while trolling and impart more action to the fly. By "retrieve" we mean that the angler uses his hands to pull the fly through the water in varying patterns of movement and pauses that are designed to attract fish. This will be discussed in greater detail later in this chapter.

Disadvantages of Trolling

One disadvantage of trolling is that, in general, one cannot use a dry fly but must fish beneath the surface. Further, while catching fish on the troll can be exciting, it is not as satisfying as catching fish by casting. The major disadvantage of trolling from a boat is that one cannot use a retrieve to attract fish unless one stops the boat. Also, when trolling from a boat by yourself and using oars, the fly rod is not in your hands;

therefore, when a fish strikes your fly you do not feel it and cannot respond quickly.

Trolling Technique

In trolling the key variable, aside from the choice of fly, is depth. Depth is determined by the speed at which the boat or tube is moving and the density of the sinking fly line.

The best depth to troll a fly is just off the bottom.

To do this in areas of fairly uniform depth adjust your speed or the length of your line until you snag bottom and then speed up a bit or take in some line. In areas of variable depth, try to keep the fly at least two feet below the surface. A good place to troll is along drop-offs. Drop-offs are those areas where the shallow water near the shore suddenly falls away to deeper water. Troll in the deeper water but near the edge of the shallower water. Most people troll too far out in the lake. Also look for drop-offs around submerged islands or around weed beds.

Because the trout's food does not move at a constant speed or in a straight line it is better to weave back and forth in your boat or tube. This will cause the fly to change depth–rising on the outside of a turn and falling deeper on the inside of the turn. Also vary your speed to make the fly rise and fall in the water column.

Troll slowly. Most beginners troll too fast. The best speed is approximately rowing speed. Rowing is a very effective trolling technique, especially if one varies the speed and pauses now and then. If trolling with an electric motor, use one with infinitely variable speed settings. This feature makes it easy to mimic the motions created by rowing–slowing down, pausing, and then speeding up.

Include retrieves in your trolling technique.

Occasionally, stop completely and let your line sink. Then pull the fly toward you in five or six short bursts followed by a pause of five or six seconds, and then repeat the pulls. Continue this until the fly is about 15 feet from the boat or tube. If this does not trigger a strike, then go back to kicking or rowing until all the retrieved line is back into the water.

When you troll let out almost the complete length of your fly line. This keeps the fly as far away from your boat or tube as possible and away from the disturbance caused by the flippers or the motor and allows your sinking line to be at its maximum depth.

Always be sure that your rod is secure, especially if you are rowing a boat. Anglers secure their rods or lines in a variety of ways. Some wrap a loop of line around their foot. Others put their foot on the butt of the rod. Some have been known to put the line in their mouths but probably the best way is to secure the rod to the boat with a bungee cord. Commercial products are also available.

Always position your rod so that the reel can free-spool. Never position the rod with the reel handle facing down where it will inhibit free-spooling.

Hold the rod at an angle to the boat or tube so that when a fish strikes, the rod can act like a shock absorber.

When I was 12 years old I had finally earned enough money cutting lawns for my neighbours to purchase my very own fly rod, reel and line. My father took me to Paul Lake where he rented a boat for himself and my brother-in-law and one, just for me. This day is imprinted in my mind as well as any home video camera could capture. The day was as pretty as they get. I had my very own rod and was in command of my very own boat, rental though it may have been. I pulled away from the lodge dock full of confidence in myself. The line was a floater and the fly a Red Bodied Carey. As I rowed I paused to pull line from the reel and trolled slowly and with great stealth over the famous Lodge shoal. As I stopped rowing to proudly hail my father, my reel began to scream and clatter about the bottom of the boat as Walter exploded in a huge towering leap behind the boat, my Red Bodied Carey firmly clamped in his monstrous jaws.

My hard worked for rod, reel and line was literally ripped from the boat. My last image of it was Walter in seemingly slow-motion jumps dragging it out to the depths of Paul Lake, where it sank from sight and remains to this day! My father, good soul that he was, consoled my sobbing grief and purchased me another rod when we passed through town on our way home. My lesson was hard learned–yours need not be. – **Gord**

Trolling Tips

- If you get a fish or a strike, turn the boat or tube and immediately go back over the same spot again–there will often be another fish there.
- Do not use a gas engine to troll because it is too noisy.

Trolling is an effective way to explore a lake and to catch fish. We believe that good trolling technique should be a part of every angler's bag of tricks.

Casting

Casting is the essence of flyfishing. It is the image of flyfishing one sees in movies and magazines. In a cast, one uses the weight of the flyline to bend the tip of the rod and as the rod straightens, it causes the line to sail out over the water. After the fly lands on the water it either floats or sinks depending on the nature of the line and the fly. The fly is retrieved and the fly is cast again.

Advantages of Casting

The major advantage of casting is that it is the best way to fish the hatches. Casting a dry fly to fish feeding on the surface is one of the most exciting experiences flyfishing has to offer. Fish often take these flies quickly with a lot of splashy action. Another advantage is that casting enables you to retrieve the fly in various ways and speeds which are attractive to fish rather than the steady pull characteristic of trolling. A third advantage is that casting allows you to remain stationary over an area where fish are feeding rather having to troll back and forth.

Casting from either a boat or tube can cover a fairly large area of water compared to the narrow strip behind the boat or tube that is covered by trolling. Casting also makes it possible to cast to rise forms or to individual fish as you see them moving around in the water to feed.

Disadvantages of Casting

The major disadvantage to casting is that it is not easy to learn. In our view, it is counter productive to try to learn to cast by reading a book and by teaching yourself. It is too easy to develop bad habits. It is for this reason that we have not included a section on how to cast. Learn to cast by having a friend who is a good caster teach you or take lessons that are offered by a local flyfishing club or through a local fly shop. In many areas night school courses on casting are available at nominal cost. After you have had some instruction, rent videos on how to cast. Note that videos assume that you will be fishing streams and will teach a number of casts designed to overcome problems caused by the currents in streams. Remember that in lakes, the water is stationary. Concentrate on learning two casts–the straight presentation cast and the roll cast.

Proper casting can be a great advantage; poor casting disturbs the water and spooks the fish. It takes some practice, but learning to cast is worth the time and effort.

Casting Tips

- Beginning anglers cast too much and spend too much time trying for another two feet of distance. Fish are caught on the retrieve–not on the cast. Keep your fly in the water as much as possible, all too often new anglers are enamoured with casting and their fly spends more time in the air than in the water. The best-kept secret in flyfishing is that your fly must be in the water to catch fish.
- Grass will not damage your fly line. Practice casting on your lawn or at a park.
- Practice while sitting in a lawn chair as if in a boat or float tube.
- Do not practice with a hook on your leader; instead, tie a small piece of yarn to your tippet. This is much safer and increases the visibility of your practice casts.
- If you are fishing from a tube you can lengthen your casts by back-peddling while you let out line and you also can begin your retrieve by a combination of back-peddling and retrieving.

Rod and Line Control

How to Hold the Rod and the Line

Whether you are casting or trolling you must have control of the rod and the line. Without proper control it is impossible to hook or land fish.

The key to successful line control lies with the hand holding the rod. Grasp the rod handle and place the line between the first two fingers of the rod hand and the rod handle. In other words, with your flyline out in the water the line passes through the guides on the rod and then is held between the first two fingers of your rod hand and the handle of the rod, and then the line goes to the reel. The grip of your fingers allows you to control the line. You should always hold the line in this position except when you are casting or stripping out line.

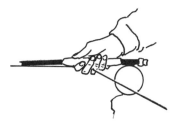

It may seem odd, but using two fingers rather than one makes it easier to control the tension on the line as it passes between your fingers and the rod handle.

Holding the line under two fingers should become habitual as it forms the basis for retrieves, setting the hook, and playing the fish. If you are trolling in a boat automatically pick up the rod and line in this way–don't let the line hang loose or you will lose control of the line and your fish as well. When retrieving a fly this grip on the line coupled with proper rod position, enables you to keep slack out of the portion of the line between the rod hand and the fly. This is important because when the line is tight it is easier to detect strikes and set the hook quickly. In playing a fish, it enables you to control the speed at which the fish takes line.

How to Strip Line Out

Letting out a lot of line quickly is known as "stripping line out". When you begin fishing, either by casting or trolling, you need to get line out into the water. Do this by grasping the leader with your line hand and pull out about a rod's length of flyline past the tip of the rod. Flip the line and leader into the water. More line can be extended by pulling it off the reel with your line hand and whipping the rod tip left to right. The action of the rod tip will pull out the line. At first you will probably be too gentle. Keep trying and you will be surprised at how the line flows out. During the process, release the line from under the fingers of your rod hand; however, as soon as the line is out to the desired length, return the line to under the first two fingers of the rod hand. Once about 15 feet of line is out, you are ready to begin to cast. If trolling, the movement of your boat or tube through the water will pull out additional line.

How to Strip Line In

"Stripping line in" means to bring in your line quickly. This is done when landing fish or when you bring in your fly to check for weeds or wind knots.

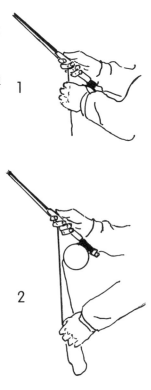

When stripping line in, do not reach ahead of your rod hand to pull in line or try to wind it on the reel. Instead, strip line in by grasping it just behind where it is held under the first two fingers of your rod hand. Pull the line through your fingers by pulling down with your line hand and arm to take in two to three feet of line with each pull.

As you strip it in, let it collect in coils that will not tangle when you want to let line out again. Mastering this stripping technique is important because, when playing a fish, you can bring in slack line quickly and, because the line is clamped between your fingers and rod handle, the line is always under your control.

Stripping line in

┌─ **Tip** ─────────────────────────────────┐

• If this is not clear, get a free lesson in line control by observing how experienced anglers handle their lines and rods.

We often see beginners who, when they hook a fish, get excited and grab the line between their rod hand and the first guide. They make one pull and wind up with the line in one hand and the rod in the other. They have no way to bring in more line without letting go of the rod. The proper technique is easy to learn. You should practice until it becomes automatic.

How to Retrieve the Fly, Detect the Take and Set the Hook

The Challenge

Finally we have come to the skills of fishing–retrieving the fly, detecting the take and setting the hook. The retrieve is pulling in the line and the fly in a manner which will cause the fish to strike at it. Sometime during the retrieve, hopefully, a fish will "strike" at or take the fly into its mouth. This is known as the "take" or a "strike". The challenge comes in detecting the take. Takes vary from a vicious strike soon after the fly hits the water to a gentle inhalation of a wet fly that is so soft it often goes unnoticed.

As soon as the take is detected, the fly must be set in the fish's mouth. Trout caught on a fly do not normally swallow a fly like fish swallow the worms you fished with as a child. The fly usually hooks in the corner of the mouth. This is the reason it is possible to catch and then release trout caught on a fly; they are not seriously harmed and will live for other anglers to enjoy.

Because the proper retrieve, detecting the take and hook setting techniques vary between dry flies and wet flies we will consider each separately.

Dry Fly Technique

Retrieves. Dry flies float on the surface and are cast with floating lines. As soon as your fly is on the water, point the rod tip directly at the fly and hold the rod so that the tip is almost touching the surface of the water. We call this the "low" rod position.

Take in enough line to remove any coils in either your line or your leader. Your first retrieve technique is to do nothing–let the fly sit for 10-15 seconds. Then, if nothing happens, twitch it a bit. If after a few twitches, nothing happens, retrieve it with a few short pulls and then wait again. As a final act before stripping the line in and casting again, pull the fly under the water and give it a few pulls. Fish seldom take dry flies close to the boat or tube, so do not retrieve all the line before recasting. (In Chapter 6 we discuss retrieves applicable to specific insects when fishing a dry fly.)

Detecting the take. Detecting the take is seldom a problem with dry flies because when a trout takes a dry fly, you can see the fish go for the fly. Fish usually take dry flies soon after they land on the water.

Setting the hook. When fishing on the surface, the instinctive reaction is to set the hook as soon as the trout is seen. This may work, but the probability is that as a beginner you will react too quickly and pull the fly out of the trout's mouth. If you are not hooking up, slow down. A fish going for a dry fly will often hook itself if you are patient. Try waiting until you can feel the strike or see the trout take the fly. Then set the hook by clamping the line to the rod handle–**remember it is being held between the rod handle and the first two fingers of the rod hand**–and quickly raise your rod with your wrist and elbow to the "middle position" which means that the rod will be roughly parallel to the water and no higher than your shoulder. We call this "clamp and set". The fish should now be securely hooked.

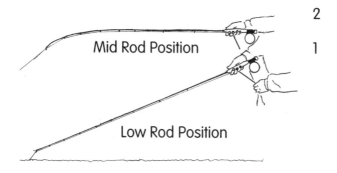

Clamp and set is a lot easier to say than to do and requires some practice. On a day when there is a lot of surface feeding and the fish are taking your fly, try retrieving with your eyes closed so that you learn to rely on feeling the take.

Wet Fly Technique

Retrieves. Wet flies are cast either with a sinking line or a floating line and are retrieved under the surface. Again, as soon as your fly is on the water, put your rod in the "low position"– the rod tip pointed directly at the fly and nearly touching the surface of the water. Take in enough line to remove any coils in either your line or your leader. When fishing with wet flies the question is what kind of action to impart to a fly that is being retrieved under the surface. Like the question of what flies to use, the issue is whether the retrieve should be "matching"– imitate the movement of a particular insect or "attraction"– provoke the fish into striking. Our view is the same one expressed with regard to flies; namely, both work.

A basic retrieve. Once the fly is in the water wait a bit to let the fly sink to where you think the fish are feeding. How fast it sinks will depend on the type of line you are using and the weight of the fly. Once the fly is in position we recommend that beginners start with a basic retrieve and then experiment to develop a suitable individual technique. (In Chapter VI we describe how each insect moves through the water and present a number of imitative retrieves.) The variables in a retrieve are the length of the pull, the speed of the pull, and the length of pauses between pulls.

Our basic retrieve consists of the following combination:
- Three 4-inch pulls,
- One 8-inch pull, and
- A pause for about a count of two.

If, after a few repetitions, this does not produce results, experiment with different pulls. Begin by varying the speed of the pulls or pause more often or for longer periods. To paraphrase Phil Rowley: "The key to successfully fishing nymphs is to change retrieves more often than patterns."

Retrieve the fly until it is about 15 feet from the boat or tube. As the fly gets closer to the boat or tube the angle of the retrieve naturally changes and the fly rises toward the surface.

Often at this point, a fish that has been following your fly will finally strike at it.

Tips

- After a cast, count to five before retrieving the fly. A cast can disturb the trout and this pause gives them a chance to return or at least turn so they are looking in the direction of the fly.
- If a trout hits your fly but does not hook up, do not jerk the fly away and cast again. Continue the retrieve and often the trout will follow the fly and hit it again. This is especially true if you are fishing leeches where the second strike can be vicious.
- Always pause during your retrieve. All insects pause or rest as they move through the water. Trout are opportunistic and seem to feed in a manner which expends the least energy. Trout will follow their prey, and attack when it pauses as this requires less effort.

The "count-down" retrieve. This is an important technique to master as it enables you to fish a fly just off the bottom and to determine the depth at which fish are feeding. This is valuable because hatches begin at the bottom of the lake and because the bigger trout feed near the bottom. Briefly stated you:

- Make your cast and let the fly sink toward the bottom for two minutes and then begin your retrieve.
- If you do not hook the bottom, increase the sinking time until you do.
- When you hook the bottom, cast again and decrease the sinking time by 15 seconds. If you do not hook the bottom you are now fishing just off the bottom.
- If after a few casts, you do not have a strike, decrease your sinking interval by 15 seconds and continue to fish closer to the surface until you find the feeding zone.

The application of this technique to chironomid fishing is described in Chapter 7.

Detecting the take. We have now come to the biggest challenge for the beginning angler–how to detect takes when fishing under the surface. In part this challenge arises from the fact that the angler cannot see the fish take the fly and must rely on "feel". If this were not enough, there is a wide variety of underwater takes.

These variations arise from the essential difference between lakes and streams. As discussed earlier, in a stream trout are stationary waiting for food to drift by. When the fish sees a fly that looks like food, it often reacts quickly and strikes at it. But, as soon as it senses that the fly is not food, it is rejected. A fish can inhale and spit out a fly very quickly. To oversimplify, trout in streams tend to strike at flies and then reject them.

This is in contrast to a lake where the water is stationary and, if the food is moving, it is moving under its own power rather than being swept along by the current.

Under these conditions fish have an additional option. Not only can they "strike and reject", they can "inspect and reject". In other words, because they have time to inspect the fly, they can reject those that do not attract them without striking them. Takes can also vary from gentle inhaling to vicious snaps depending on the speed the food source is moving.

The variety of takes means that the wet fly angler must watch the line very carefully. Often you can detect a take by the slight movement in the line where it enters the water. Keeping the rod and the line pointed at the fly and eliminating the coils in the line will help you feel and see a take.

At other times you will feel a strong tug on the line leaving no doubt that a fish has hit it. You will also sometimes feel a pecking at the fly which indicates that the fish is following the fly.

Setting the hook. How do beginners respond to this variety of underwater takes? The short answer is too late and too forcefully.

In part, this may be because the take was not felt–either because it was so soft or because the line and leader were so slack that the feel of the take never reached the angler's hands. Alternatively, the take was felt, but the reaction to it was too slow and by the time the hook was "set", the fish was off.

A slow reaction to a take often occurs because the beginning angler makes a decision rather than simply reacting. Then, once the decision is made, the beginning angler over-reacts by jerking the rod. This either pulls the fly out of the trout's mouth or breaks off the fly.

Setting the hook in wet fly fishing is the same as in dry fly fishing–clamp the line to the rod and quickly lift the rod to the middle position.

Many of my clients are new to flyfishing but have a fishing background using spinning or level wind casting reels and have fished for Bass and other species where the hook set is fast and strong. This definitely does not work when flyfishing for trout! When Bass fishing the leader or monofilament line is much heavier and when they apply this force on their first few trout on a fly rod my supply of carefully tied flies suffers worse losses than the stock market. My favourite example of flies lost to hook sets happened with four great guys from Tennessee–all Bass fisherman on their first flyfishing trip. Their first day found us in the middle of a great Mayfly hatch and my supply of flies was being rapidly depleted. To get their attention and hopefully to tame down their wild hook setting, I announced that yes the first two flies where provided as part of my guide services but that the third fly lost to a fish on the hook set was $5 US and that subsequent flies where $50 US each. I was kidding of course but it did get their attention and no more flies where lost to vicious hook setting techniques. Strike gently but firmly! **– Gord**

Feel. What the beginning angler lacks is "feel". The question is how to develop the feel required to detect takes and set the hook. Instruction–whether books, classes or videos–will not do it. Feel will only come with experience. What follows is a way to learn from experience. More accurately, it is a way to learn from your mistakes.

- In a retrieve always be prepared to "clamp and set"–clamp the line to the rod handle and raise the rod to the middle position.
- Whenever you feel any resistance to your retrieve–clamp and set.
- If you do not hook up at all, try to react more quickly.
- If you have the fish on and it gets off right away, try to strike more forcefully.
- If you have the fish on and you pull the fly out of the fish's mouth or break off the fly, try to strike less forcefully.

Do not become discouraged if at first you have problems detecting and reacting to underwater takes. This requires experience and, in the next chapter, we tell you how to get that experience. Resign yourself to the fact that you probably will not hook the first five or six fish that take your fly. Once you have caught your first trout, the second one will be much easier. Develop your underwater retrieval skills because that is where most fish feed and are caught. We estimate that 90 per cent of the fish we catch are caught on flies fished under the surface.

Tips

- Small fish strike quicker than large fish.
- Always be prepared to set the hook. If you feel any resistance–**clamp and set**. This may result in some false positives (weeds) but this is better than missing a fish.
- Do not respond to a take that feels like a "pull" by pulling back. Always clamp and set.
- Sometimes a take can be seen by a slight backward movement in a tight line. If so, clamp and set.

How to Land the Fish

Playing The Fish

Hopefully you have successfully hooked your fish. Now you have to play the fish until it is tired enough that you can bring it to the boat or tube. Again rod control is the key to success.

With the hook set and your rod in the mid position (roughly parallel to the water and no higher than your shoulder), you are able to play the fish on your terms. The mid-position coupled

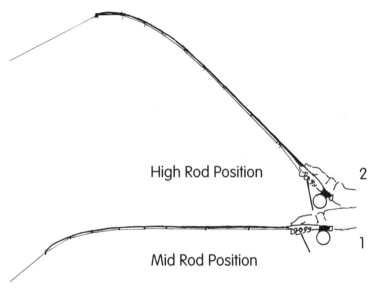

High Rod Position   2

Mid Rod Position   1

with clamping the line in your rod hand allows you to control the fish. Now there are two scenarios that can occur.

The first is if the fish decides to run toward you, as they often do. Raise the rod to where it is pointed at about 11 o'clock –the "high" rod position.

Maintain pressure on the fish and begin stripping in line. In a tube, strip line and peddle backwards as fast as possible.

The second is if the fish decides to run away from you. Keep your rod in the mid-position. Let the fish take line out through your fingers. Letting the line run out through the "clamp" in your rod hand lets you control the speed the line is taken so that you remain in control. When the run is complete and the fish swims back toward you there will be slack in the line. When this happens raise the rod to the high-position and strip in line. If you have hooked Walter he may run far enough to take you into the backing. When that happens, as soon as you have slack line, reel in as much backing as possible because he is likely to run again. Try to play the fish with the fly line rather than the backing.

During the first stage when the fish is running do not try to slow or stop it. If you try to stop the fish by clamping or holding the line it will break the tippet and you will lose both the fish and the fly. When the fish is running let it do what it wants but maintain control of the line. When the fish stops to rest or turns you will feel the pressure go off of the rod and the rod tip will straighten. When you feel the pressure go off of the rod that is the time to strip in line. Keep the line tight at all times. If there is slack in the line the fish will escape. Playing a fish is usually a series of runs which take out line followed by pauses or slack line when you can strip line in. Strip line in with long pulls of your line hand but don't let go of the line that is clamped to the rod handle. The bigger and stronger the fish the more times it will run with your line. Each time you strip in line the fish will be closer to the boat or tube. Stand up if you are in a boat because this permits longer strips of line and more leverage to control the movement of the fish. Keep this up until the fish tires enough so that you have control over it and can bring it in.

Tips

- Always keep a very light drag on your reel. In lake fishing use just enough drag to keep the spool from "free-spooling" when you cast. Free spooling will cause your line to snarl inside your reel.
- If the fish jumps out of the water and high into the air–take up slack; however, be prepared to let line out if, after the fish is back in the water, it decides to run away from you.
- Never raise the rod so high that the tip is behind your head. If the rod is this far back, it is difficult to control the line and you probably will lose the fish.

This little lesson in losing big fish is locked in my brain forever. I was guiding a delightful couple from the eastern US a few years back, we were on one of my walk-in lakes fishing from pontoon boats for very large trout during a Caddis hatch. The large trout were savaging the big Caddis and the sounds of the takes could be heard all over the lake. When Sally (name changed to protect the semi-innocent) broke off yet another monster trout I paddled over beside her to tie on another fly. I gently suggested that she allow the fish to run. She, without hesitation, said "Oh no, I never let them run because they could get away". I asked how many large trout she normally landed. The reply, of course, was none! We then had a brief practice session where I pretended to be the fish and paddled furiously backwards doing my best running trout imitation all the while pleading with her to allow line to be released from her death grip. After the lesson, it was back to angling and she landed Walter–a beautiful six pound fish. She had let the fish run! To land large trout or even small fish with shoulders and an attitude, you must allow them to take line on a run. If you don't, you had better have a large supply of flies as they will break off time and time again. **– Gord**

Bringing the Fish In

Once you have control over the fish, strip in the line using the rod as a lever to guide the fish toward your boat or tube. Bring the fish in as rapidly as possible; especially, if you plan to release it. Assuming the fish is large enough, the final phase is netting it. Hold the net still and guide the fish headfirst into it. Do not try to catch the fish with the net by swishing it around in the water. This frightens the fish and may cause it to make another run. This usually results in the fish breaking off because while handling the net you are not in a good position to control either the rod or the line. Once it is in the net, you will either release the fish or bring it in to keep.

Keeping Fish

If you decide to keep a fish, kill it quickly by a blow to the head. Do not put it on a stringer or in a pan of water. Keeping fish in water, especially warm water, softens the flesh and destroys their table qualities. Instead cover them with a wet towel so that the evaporation will cool them or put them in a cooler.

Cleaning Fish

Trout are easy to clean. There is no need to scrape scales or cut off fins. All you have to do is:

- Hold the fish belly up in one hand.
- With the other hand insert the knife in the anal vent and slice the belly all the way to the head.
- Cut off the head including the gills.
- Strip everything out of the abdominal cavity.
- Break the membrane along the spine with your thumb and strip out the spleen which is the dark strip you will see next to the backbone.
- Rinse.

Note–In the Province of British Columbia, if you are going to transport trout, you must leave on both the head and tail for size and species identification. Consult the regulations in your own jurisdiction.

Tips

- There is an easy way to clean fish and leave the heads on. It involves cutting through the jaw and over the tongue. It is easy to do but difficult to describe. If you see someone do it, ask them to show you how.
- Refrigerate or freeze cleaned trout as soon as you can.

Releasing Fish

If you wish to release the fish keep it in the water and remove the fly by reaching down and grasping the fly with your fingers or with your forceps and give it a backward twist. Gently hold the fish in the water until it shows a good bit of strength to swim away. If it does not appear to be recovering then gently move it back and forth to create a gentle water flow through its gills.

Always release spawners. Conservation questions aside, there is no sport in catching spawning fish as their vitality has been sapped. Besides that, they don't taste good.

Photographing Fish

If you wish a photo of your trout do so as quickly as possible and follow these simple rules:

• Wet your hands before touching the trout. The slime or mucus that coats their body is for their protection. Dry hands or excessive handling will destroy this protective film and may cause the fish to become infected.

• When you lift the fish for your photo, support the body with both hands and do not squeeze. Fish are supported in the water by natural buoyancy. When removed from the water their internal organs must be supported.

• Take your photo quickly and return the fish to water immediately.

Comments on Barbless Hooks

We recommend the use of barbless hooks whether or not it is required by law. It has been our experience that you don't lose fish on barbless fishhooks except when you fail to keep a tight line. More importantly, barbless hooks are easier to remove from a fish and certainly are less injurious to them. Fish have only a small amount of blood and a bleeding fish will seldom survive–especially if it is a small fish.

┌─**Tips**────────────────────────────────

• Check the regulations. In some waters, catch and release or barbless hooks may be mandatory.

• The flies you buy probably will have barbs. Use the smooth jaws of your forceps to bend down the barbs.

Closing Comments

You will have noticed that we place a lot of emphasis on proper rod position. In our opinion rod position separates successful anglers from those who simply spend a nice day on the lake.

Many of my clients are either inexperienced or are stream anglers. They are lake flyfishing for the first time and they usually hold their rods too high.

It is worth repeating the key elements to correct rod position for lake flyfishing–whether fishing from a tube or a boat:

- *When you have completed the cast the rod should be in the **low position**–the tip of the rod almost touching the water's surface and pointed at the fly.*
- *Strip in enough line to remove any coils in either your fly line or your leader. This simple process puts you into immediate contact with your fly.*

*By having the rod pointed at the fly just off the water surface you are ready for the take or strike and when this occurs you set the hook by simply raising your wrist and arm to a **mid position**–roughly parallel and no higher than your shoulder.*

We have observed that beginners often fail to set the hook because they hold the rod too high. This can also lead to inattention. All too often I see anglers, obviously in La La Land, the rod moving higher and higher as they daydream. Guess what, the long awaited strike, of course, and another LDR (Long Distance Release–another way to say "you lost the fish"). A proper low rod position creates a focal point, in that you are watching the end of the rod and the first few feet of line. You are focused and when the take does come, a simple lift of the wrist and success!

*When I teach new fly anglers I spend time with them on a lawn going through the basics of casting, but I also spend almost as much time working on the fishing rod position, the hook set and playing the fish by either stripping or reeling. Strangers watching might think me completely mad because when I teach "playing the fish" I act as the fish. I hold their leader and run about as a fish might. If it is a couple or a group, I have everyone take turns being The Fish. When a real fish strikes, they are not surprised. Line control and proper rod position are already a habit. – **Gord***

Chapter 5

Your First Day

5. YOUR FIRST DAY

You now have an understanding of the basic skills, you have bought a fishing license and you have read the regulations. It is time to go fishing and learn how to fish your all-purpose patterns.

Choose a Lake

You must first choose a lake. The number and average size of the trout vary from lake to lake. Contrary to popular belief, large fish are not necessarily found in large lakes or in remote lakes. The mass of fish that can be supported in any lake depends upon the total amount of food available. Put another way, given the amount of food available, a lake can support either many small fish or fewer large fish. Thus, fishing pressure tends to result in larger fish and the natural increase from spawning tends to result in smaller fish. Remote lakes get less fishing pressure. This, plus the natural increase through spawning, can result in many very small fish–a process called "alpenizing". On the other hand, lakes popular with anglers receive substantial fishing pressure and, if this is in balance with the natural increase and planting, the result can be a substantial population of good-sized fish.

We recommend that, at first, the beginner angler choose a relatively small lake with a substantial population of smaller fish–eight to 12 inches.

These lakes can provide lots of action and the opportunity to develop fishing skills. To find one, ask a local fly shop for advice or for a publication that describes fishing opportunities in the area.

Make a Plan

Every time you go out on a lake you are going to act on answers to the following questions:
- Are the fish feeding today?
- If so, where and on what?
- What fly should I use and how should I present it?

Someone else may answer these questions for you, but you are still acting on them. Our point is simple. Rather than rushing out onto the lake, take time to consider these questions and make tentative answers–make a plan–then go out on the lake and test it. Be prepared to modify your plan as you get more information or if conditions change.

Troll Around the Lake

You have now arrived at the lake and there are no other anglers to observe. You don't see any fish moving or any rise forms. You can't see any insects coming off the water nor do you see any birds feeding on insects. Since you can't see any evidence of feeding or hatches you must base your plan on presentation techniques. We recommend that you begin by trolling.

From the shore, study the structure of the lake. Look for shoals–the shallow areas of the lake. Note any points of land extending into the lake and any bays. Judge the water depth by looking at the slope of the land next to the lake; for example, a bluff on the lake shore usually means deep water and flat lake shore suggests a shoal extending into the lake. Look for outlets and inlets. Look for vegetation growing up out of the water– these weed beds may be extensive or just a fringe along the shore. Look for islands and "submerged" islands–humps of land that peak just below the surface of the water–which are usually indicated by offshore weed beds.

LAKE STRUCTURE

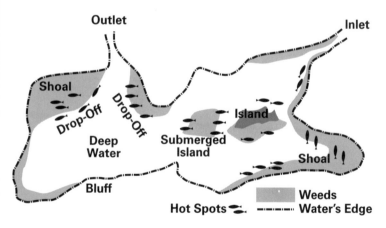

Once you have the structure of the lake in mind, move out into the lake until you are over the line between shallow water where you can see the bottom and the darker deep water where you can't see the bottom. Troll along this line in the direction you think shoals are likely to occur. Start with your Woolly Bugger on a Type II sinking line with the recommended 9 foot 4X leader. Plan to troll around the entire lake and if there is no action when you are about half way around, change from your Woolly Bugger to your Doc Spratley.

During this tour of the lake begin to develop your powers of observation by looking for:
- "hot spots"
- signs of insect activity
- signs of feeding fish.

Look for Hot Spots

As you tour the lake, continue to study the structure of the lake and look for "hot spots". Hot spots are those sites, which meet the trout's three requirements of oxygen, food and cover. The key is to ask yourself the following question: if I were a shy but hungry trout in need of oxygen–where would I hide? There are two general answers. The first is along the shoreline in spots with good cover and access to cool water.

The most important of these are the shoals and the drop-offs that connect them to the deeper water. The shoals are an abundant source of all the trout's food chain. Approximately 80 per cent of a trout's feeding takes place in water from two to 15 feet deep–the depth provided by shoals. The drop-offs at the edge of shoals are vital to the trout's security. When they are foraging for food in shallow water they are exposed to their predators and when threatened they can move quickly to the shelter of the deep water at the drop-off. Trout spend the majority of their time cruising the area of the drop-off waiting for a major hatch to occur on the shoals or for the cover provided by clouds or a wind riffle so they can return to feeding on the shoal.

Not all shoals have drop-offs and not all drop-offs are next

PROFILE OF LAKE STRUCTURE

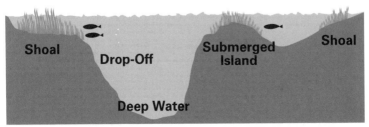

Shoal Drop-Off Submerged Island Shoal Deep Water

to shoals. Some shoals gradually extend into the deep water and drop-offs also occur next to islands and submerged islands.

Other areas which provide good cover and access to cool water include:

- open channels between or around weed beds,
- deep water next to islands,
- submerged islands, and
- submerged structure out from the shore such as sunken trees.

Also look for fish in spots with more oxygen, either because the water is cooler or because it has been oxygenated through wave action. These include the areas near underwater springs and in deep water close to where streams enter the lake.

Tips

- Fish are not evenly distributed throughout a lake, they stay only in those areas which meet their habitat requirements. Large portions of the lake will not meet the key requirements and are known as "dead water". A common error made by beginners is to troll in the middle of the lake. Unless there is a submerged island or a spring, the middle of the lake is probably dead water. Do not spend time over the deep water in the middle of the lake unless you see fish rising. Instead, concentrate on the potential hot spots.
- Begin by trolling along the edges of the drop-offs. If this is not productive, go to other areas such as bays or points of land with long shoals extending out into the lake.

Look for Insect Activity

As you tour the lake, look for signs of insect activity. Your first objective is to develop your ability to identify insects. If you see insects coming off the surface of the water try to identify them. In open water they will be chironomids, mayflies or caddis adults. Along the shore they will be dragonflies or damselflies. Compare what you see with the descriptions in Chapter 2.

Look for "shucks". These are the external casings left behind by emerging insects. Chironomids, the mayfly, and the caddisfly will leave shucks on the water surface. The chironomid shuck will have white gill tufts, the mayfly shuck will have three long tails and the caddis shuck will be tubular and considerably larger than either of the others. Look for dragonfly shucks on structures of exposed rocks near the shoreline and for damselfly shucks on the reeds near the shore.

Watch the birds. Birds feed on hatching insects. Look for swallows dipping down and taking insects off the water. This usually indicates a chironomid hatch. Look for birds "roosting" on the reeds and taking insects. Often the bird is a blackbird and the insect a damselfly. Look for diving ducks. The insects they knock off weeds will be taken by trout.

Tip

- If you see hatching insects or shucks, troll through the area. You may want to change your plan and try casting.

Look for Signs of Feeding Fish

Sometimes when trout feed on or near the surface, you can see them. Other times you can only see the "rise forms" they have left behind. Trout take an insect by inhaling it and letting the water out through their gills. When a trout takes an insect off the surface it leaves a ring which has an air bubble in it caused by the fact that the trout also inhaled a bit of air. When a trout takes an insect just below the surface, it creates a bulge in the water surface, which leaves a ring without an air bubble.

Tips

- When a trout jumps straight out of the water and flops back in, the trout is not feeding. It is attempting to shake small parasites out of its gills. Although these trout are not feeding it does indicate to you that fish are in that area and are active.
- If you see signs of feeding fish, troll through the area. You may want to try casting.

Review Your Plan

After you have made a tour around the lake, you should review your plan (if you have not already done so). You may have had enough success that you decide to continue trolling. Alternatively, you may want to do some casting–either because you want to practice or because of what you observed on your tour of the lake. If you have been fortunate enough to observe a hatch or lots of feeding fish, you would be foolish not to change your plan. Survey chapters 2 and 6 and try to figure out what is happening and do your best.

Let us assume that you want to try casting.

Cast Toward a Weed Bed

In your tour of the lake you certainly saw some weed beds–masses of aquatic vegetation that grow in the water and are usually close to shore–and probably saw signs of smaller fish feeding among the weeds.

Return to this area and anchor so that you can cast comfortably to the edge of the weed bed. Use a floating line with the standard 9 foot 4X leader and, at first, put on your dry fly–the "Humpy". Put floatant on it and cast it to the edge of the weed bed and retrieve it with our recommended dry fly technique. One can almost always catch small fish in these locations. If not, try another weed bed. However, catching fish is not your only objective. This is the ideal situation to practice your dry fly retrieve, to learn about how fish take a fly on the surface and to learn how to set the hook. If you can see the fish, watch what they do when the fly lands on the water and how they move to inspect it before striking.

Assuming you are raising fish, change your fly. Take off the Humpy and put on the Halfback. You will now be fishing a wet fly just below the surface with a floating line. Practice your underwater retrieves. Start with the basic retrieve and experiment.

Cast Over a 'Hot Spot'

If after a while you have had enough of casting toward the
weeds or if you are not raising fish, move to a hot spot. In your
tour of the lake you should have spotted one of the prime hot
spots–a shoal with a drop-off connecting it to deeper water. Go
back there and anchor.

An important question is how to best position your boat or
tube relative to the shoal and the drop-off. As you might expect
it is always determined by our friend and enemy–the wind.

The general rule for fishing hot spots is that when there is a
breeze on the water, always position yourself upwind of the
feeding zone.

Trout will always turn their heads into the waves because
the breeze and the waves are drifting the food to them.
Accordingly, make your cast to allow your fly to drift naturally
into the feeding zone. If you are a right-handed caster,
whenever possible, position yourself so that you cast with the
wind off your left shoulder. This will keep the cast fly away
from your head.

When fishing drop-offs, the ideal situation is a breeze from
the shoal toward the drop-off. In this case anchor half a cast
inside the shoal so that you cast with the wind and into the
deeper water. Retrieve back onto the shoal with the majority of
your retrieve following the profile of the grade of the drop-off
from deep to shallow. This presents the fly with maximum
effect.

A more common situation has the wind coming from the
deep water toward the shoal. In this situation, anchor at the
edge of the drop-off or just outside. Cast along the edge of the
drop-off quartering into the wind. Retrieve along the edge of

the shoal from deep to shallow to keep the fly in the deep water as long a possible.

Once you are in position, use whatever sinking line you decided to buy (Intermediate or Type II) with the standard 9 foot 4X leader. First put on your Halfback pattern and cast it as recommended above. Again, practice your underwater retrieves. Start with the basic retrieve and experiment. After awhile, change to your Doc Spratley and continue to practice your retrieve.

Check Your Equipment

Periodically throughout the day you should check your equipment.
- Check your rod to be sure the sections still fit together snugly. If not, tighten them. Casting with a loose ferrule can cause a rod to break.
- Check your hook and, if it is bent, straighten it a bit or replace it. Weeds, snags and even hooking a fish can bend a hook and fish seldom hook up on a bent hook.
- Clean off any weeds on your hook. Trout are seldom fooled by a garland of weeds.
- Check your leader for length and for "wind knots". As we have discussed earlier wind knots weaken a leader and we would hate to have you break off in Walter because of a wind knot. (You may wonder what happens to all the hooks Walter must have in his mouth. Given the acidity of a trout's mouth, they quickly rust away.)

Review Your Day

Accomplishments

It has been a long day. Let's review what you have accomplished. You have:
- learned how to explore a new lake
- presented flies by trolling
- presented flies by casting both on the surface and under the surface
- tested all the flies in your fly box
- practiced your retrieves
- practiced detecting strikes and setting the hook
- begun to identify insects
- learned how to position your boat or tube.

Hopefully, you will have caught fish. Even if you have not, you have had a worthwhile day and maybe next time you will catch Walter.

If you have enough time and energy after you have come off the water, increase your knowledge of insects by:
- going to the windward side of the lake and looking for shucks the wind will have blown to the shore
- looking on the underside of your boat or tube where you are apt to find leeches
- look along the shore where you are apt to find leeches, shrimp and caddis larva
- turning over rocks and logs where you are apt to find dragonfly nymphs and shrimp
- look in the weeds, for nymphs.

Note what you see and using the illustrations in Chapter 2, develop your insect identification skills.

> ## Tip
> - As you become more experienced you will want to make these observations before you go out on the lake so you will be prepared to select your pattern to match the food in the lake.

Make a Record

It is time to start a fishing diary. Record what you want to remember about this lake–for example, the hot spots, insects observed, flies used, and fish caught. Record the date and the weather. Over time, these records will be a valuable guide.

Other Anglers

In our idealized version of your first day, we made the assumption that you were the only angler on the lake. This happens, but more often there are other anglers at a lake, not all of whom are flyfishing. The presence of other anglers offers both opportunities and responsibilities.

The major opportunity is that other anglers may provide information concerning the questions to be answered when forming your plan–are the fish feeding and, if so where and on what? One way is to ask those on the shore–anglers or their spouses–whether anything is happening. Another is to observe other flyfishers who are on the lake. Note where they are and get as close to them as courtesy permits.

This brings us to your responsibility to other anglers. Other anglers consider where they are fishing a hot spot or they would not be there. Your first responsibility is not to crowd in. The rule of thumb is to leave about 100 feet (two cast lengths) between anglers. Anglers who know each other may fish closer, but you should not be closer than about 100 feet unless invited in. Also, stay away from the area behind casting anglers because the line goes as far behind the caster on the back cast as it goes forward and good casters throw the line a long way.

Your second responsibility is to enter and exit the area of the hot spot as unobtrusively as you can. Do not power in or out unless you have an electric motor. Lower your anchors gently and try not to lash the water with your casts.

Watch those who are catching fish and try to figure out what they are doing. Listen to what they are saying to each other–you will probably learn what the successful angler is using.

Tip

- Do not ask a direct question such as "what are you using?" This is not considered good form and you probably will not get an honest answer. Instead, give it a try on your own. Demonstrate that you need help and it probably will be volunteered. If not, ask an indirect question such as, "I'm not doing very well–do you have any suggestions?"

Closing Comments

The approach described in this section as your "first day" is how we fish a lake for the first time. I have a mania for fishing new lakes and have fished over 100 lakes in British Columbia. I recommend you use the technique described in this chapter whenever you fish a lake for the first time. It was only after I retired and moved to Kamloops that I began fishing a few lakes more intensely–which is another way to describe the next chapter. **– Ken**

Chapter 6

Fishing Imitative Patterns

6. FISHING IMITATIVE PATTERNS

The plan of the "first day" should be repeated until you have confidence in your skills and become interested in fishing with more imitative patterns. Before you begin, you will have to buy the imitative patterns and learn more about identifying insects. After discussing these topics, we recommend how to fish these patterns at the time of the year when the foods they represent are most important in the trout's diet. The fishing season runs from ice-off to freeze-up, but in terms of what fish eat, there are four distinct periods. The first is "early season", which runs from ice-off to when the hatches begin. Next is "prime time"–the period after the water warms and the hatches and emergences occur. Then, in the summer, are the "doldrums" when water temperatures are highest. Finally, there is "late season" when the water temperatures have cooled again. This period lasts until freeze-up.

Selecting the Imitative Patterns

The Modest (but adequate) Fly Box

When you are ready to fish with more imitative patterns, we recommend that you buy the following patterns and sizes.

INSECT	FLY PATTERN	SIZE
Shrimp	Werner's Shrimp (olive)	10
Leech	Marabou Leech (black)	8
Dragonfly nymph	Dragonfly nymph (olive)	6
Damselfly nymph	Damselfly nymph (golden)	12
Mayfly nymph	Pheasant Tail Nymph	12
Mayfly dun	Adams (gray)	14
Caddisfly pupa	Carey Special (green body)	10
Caddisfly adult	Adult caddisfly (green body)	8

These flies are generally available in fly shops and are pictured in colour in the centre of this book. If the exact patterns we recommend are not available from your local fly shop, do not hesitate to accept recommendations for a substitute. The point is to resist excessive accumulation.

Bead-head Flies

Recently, bead-head flies have appeared. These are conventional patterns, but with a metallic bead just behind the eye of the hook. The flies are effective–in part because of increased attractiveness and in part because the increased weight causes them to sink faster. We have not specified bead-head flies but, if they are available in the appropriate patterns, buy them.

Insect Identification

Once the imitative patterns are in your fly box, the next step is to learn more about identifying insects. In our concept of a plan, a key question is "are the fish feeding today, and if so, on what?" One way to answer this question is to examine the stomach contents of fish that have already been caught by others–either by watching them clean their fish or by offering to clean the fish for them. A better way is to use a "stomach pump". This pump is similar to a turkey baster and is badly named. It should be called an "esophagus pump" because, if it is used properly, it extracts without injury to the fish only what has been eaten recently and is still in the esophagus–not the decomposed contents of the stomach. It is worth buying a pump.

A stomach pump shows what trout are eating

How to Use a Pump

- Bring the fish to the net as quickly as possible; keep the fish in the net and in the water.
- Remove the fly.
- Wet your hands and turn the fish upside down (this calms the fish).
- Put the pump in the water and depress and release the bulb a couple of times to flush and wet the pump. Do not fill the bulb with water as per the package instructions.
- Depress the empty bulb slightly and with a gentle twisting motion insert the tube into the trout's mouth.
- Continue with a very slight pressure until you feel resistance. The tube is now in the esophagus.
- Release the pressure on the bulb and extract the pump from the fish at the same time.
- Set the bulb aside.
- Release the trout.
- Expel the contents of the pump into a small container.

You can now study what the trout has eaten most recently and choose an appropriate fly pattern of the correct size and colour.

Tip

- Do not pump small fish (15 inches or less). It is too hard on them.

How to Fish Imitative Patterns in the Early Season

Early season is from ice-off until the hatches start. This is the time to fish shrimp and leeches and, to a lesser extent, dragonfly and damselfly nymphs.

How to Fish Shrimp Patterns in the Early Season

Shrimp live close to the bottom and are more active at night or when light levels are low. They swim about six to 12 inches at a time and then stop. When stopped, they sink toward the bottom, usually in a curled position. The swimming and sinking movements are erratic–not rhythmic. Trout with their tails up digging in the weeds are feeding on shrimp

Casting technique. Early in the season, as the water

warms, shrimp become active and will be found in the weed-grown shallows close to the bottom.

- The appropriate fly is your size 10 olive Werner's Shrimp.
- Use a floating line with the standard 9 foot 4X leader plus 3 feet of 4X tippet to create a 12-foot leader.
- Cast and let the fly sink to an appropriate depth. The objective is to keep the fly close to the bottom or to the weed tips and to move it in a manner that suggests the erratic movement of the shrimp.
- The retrieve should be short rapid pulls with frequent stops of about 5 seconds. Shrimp glide when they move to protective cover, so throw in a longer, slower pull during your retrieve. Do not use a rhythmic retrieve.
- Strikes may come at any time, but are more likely to come during the pause between pulls.

Trolling technique. Trolling a shrimp pattern can be a very effective technique in the early season.

- The appropriate fly is your size 10 olive Werner's Shrimp.
- Use a Type II sinking line with a 9 foot 4X leader and slow down until you catch on a weed and then speed up a bit or shorten your line.
- Occasionally stop and retrieve your fly in the manner described above.

How to Fish Leech Patterns in the Early Season

Leeches are bottom dwellers and prefer a bottom with a mix of stones and debris–not sand or mud. Leeches are most active nocturnally; however, they can be observed swimming in open water during daylight. They swim in an undulating up-and-down motion. Fish prefer small leeches–about one and a half inches–especially in daylight.

Casting technique. Leeches are found along the shoreline wherever there is cover; however, in the early season, leeches can be found swimming at all depths.

- The appropriate flies are either your size 8 olive Woolly Bugger or your size 8 black marabou leech.
- Use either a floating line or Intermediate line, depending on depth, with the standard nine-foot 4X leader.
- Cast and let the fly sink to the appropriate depth, which in the early season is rather shallow–from two to 10 feet of water.
- The objective is to move the pattern across the path of any feeding fish in a manner that suggests the undulating

MINIMAL FLY BOX

**Black
Doc Spratley
with a silver rib**

**Olive
Woolly Bugger**

Halfback

**Humpy
with a black body**

MODEST BUT ADEQUATE FLY BOX

Werner's Shrimp (olive)

Marabou Leech (black)

Dragonfly nymph

Damselfly nymph

MODEST BUT ADEQUATE FLY BOX

Pheasant Tail nymph

Adams

Carey Special (green)

Adult Caddis (green)

CHIRONOMID PUPA

**Black
Chironomid**

**Black Bead Head
Chironomid**

CLIPPED FLIES

Clipped Woolly Bugger

Clipped Spratley

movement of a leech. First try a retrieve of long slow pulls of about 12 inches followed by a pause. If, after a while, there is no response, change to a retrieve of a few short strips of about three inches followed by a pause.

- Strikes can be unusually hard and may come immediately or, more typically, close to the boat. If the strikes are "short"– the fish does not hook up–continue the retrieve. Often the trout's second strike will be violent. If the trout breaks off, put on a stronger tippet.

Trolling technique. In the early season, because leeches can be found in open water, a leech pattern is an excellent trolling pattern.

- The appropriate flies are either your size 8 olive Woolly Bugger or your size 8 black marabou leech.
- Use a Type II sinking line with a 9 foot 4X leader.
- Troll along the shore or over the drop-offs.

How to Fish Dragonfly Patterns in the Early Season

Dragonfly nymphs are available to trout year-round. On a daily basis, the nymphs are most available during their active feeding period which is at dawn, dusk or at night–the same time when their natural prey, shrimp, are most active. They are active swimmers and move by propelling water through the tip of the abdomen. Usually these nymphs move slowly, but can move very quickly in short bursts.

As explained in Chapter 2, there are two types of dragonflies: weed dwellers and mud dwellers. We recommend that beginning anglers concentrate on fishing with the larger weed dweller patterns.

Accordingly, our recommendations as to technique and fly patterns pertain only to the weed dweller.

Casting technique. When dragonfly nymphs are not migrating to the shore to emerge, dragonfly patterns should be fished along a shoal or drop off.

- The appropriate fly is your size 6 olive Dragonfly nymph, although you can try your size 10 Halfback. In the early season, dragonfly nymphs are larger than in the rest of the season because they are ready to emerge. After emergence, the average size of the remaining dragonfly nymphs is smaller as they will not emerge until next year.
- Use a floating or Intermediate line, depending on the water depth, with the standard 9 foot 4X leader.
- Cast parallel to the shoal and let the fly sink until it is just off

the bottom. If there is no response cast out into deeper water or toward the shore.

- The objective is to move the pattern along the bottom in a manner that suggests the occasional short movements of the dragonfly nymph. Retrieve with very short, slow pulls interspersed with frequent pauses. Occasionally throw in a slow long pull or let the pattern rest on the bottom.
- Strikes can occur at any time and tend to be soft in shallow water and hard in deeper water. If you are not hooking up on soft takes, you may be pulling the fly out of the fish's mouth. Try responding to a soft take by "clamping" and lifting your rod more slowly to the middle position.

Trolling technique. Trolling a dragonfly pattern is also an effective technique in the early season.

- The appropriate flies are both your size 10 halfback and your size 6 olive Dragonfly nymph.
- Use a Type II sinking line with a 9 foot 4X leader.
- Occasionally stop and retrieve your fly in the manner described above.
- Watch your rod tip closely. If there is any tip movement, stop rowing, pick up your rod, and make a gentle retrieve. Be prepared to react to a strike.

How to Fish Damselfly Patterns in the Early Season

Large damselfly populations are associated with lakes having abundant vegetation and the nymphs are commonly found along the edges of the lake in water ranging from a few inches deep to 10 feet.

The damselfly nymph uses its broad tail-like gills to wiggle through the water. The forward movement is slow with frequent rests.

Casting technique. In the early season damselfly nymphs are to be found along the shoreline in shallow water. They are immature and therefore smaller than later in the season.

- The appropriate fly is your size 12 golden Damselfly nymph.
- Use a floating line with the standard 9 foot 4X leader or an Intermediate line with the same leader.
- Cast along the shore parallel to the reeds or tullies.
- The objective is to imitate the slow wiggle of the nymph. Retrieve in short pulls with occasional short pauses.
- Strikes can occur at any time but are apt to occur during the pauses.

Trolling technique. Because damselfly nymphs are along

the shore in the early season, it is necessary to use a slightly different trolling technique.

- The appropriate fly is your size 12 golden damselfly nymph.
- But use the same leader and lines as for casting–a standard 9 foot 4X leader on either a floating or an Intermediate line.
- Troll as close to the shore as possible and keep the fly close to the surface.

How to Fish Imitative Patterns During Emergences and Hatches

The period when the dragon and damselfly nymphs emerge and the chironomids, mayflies and sedges hatch is known as "prime time". This section discusses appropriate techniques for each of these insects as well as shrimp and leeches during prime time.

How to Fish Dragonfly Patterns During an Emergence

The dragonfly emergence. Dragonfly nymphs are available to trout all season long and trout like them because they are large and provide a lot of food for little exertion.

However, trout feed most actively on dragonfly nymphs during the spring emergence.

The emergence is the action of an individual dragonfly nymph and is not a mass migration as occurs in a damselfly emergence.

Developed nymphs migrate to shore and crawl up on vegetation to emerge as an adult. Wing pads of the nymphs darken in coloration just prior to emergence. The emergence begins in July and is normally from early morning to midday.

Casting technique. When the dragonfly nymph emerges, it moves from deep water toward shore where it crawls out of the water and the insect breaks from its external skeleton to emerge as an adult dragonfly.

- The appropriate fly is your size 6 olive Dragonfly nymph.
- Use an Intermediate line with the standard 9 foot 4X leader or a Type II sinking line with the same leader.
- Anchor the boat on the shoal at the edge of the drop off and cast out over the drop off into deeper water.
- Use the count-down method to get the fly to the bottom.
- The objective is to move the pattern in a manner that suggests the dragonfly nymph's propulsion toward the shore. First try a medium slow retrieve of about six-inch pulls

interspersed with short pauses. If after a while, this does not work, add a sharp tug at the end of each pull.

- Takes will occur at any time but usually on a pause.

Trolling technique. Dragonfly nymphs are good trolling patterns during prime time. Use the same equipment and technique as in the early season except, if you stop to retrieve, use the retrieve described above–medium slow six-inch pulls followed by a pause.

How to Fish Damselfly Patterns During an Emergence

The damselfly emergence. Damselfly nymphs are available to trout year-round but the most active feeding is during their emergence.

It is often a mass migration beginning in the mid-morning and continuing into the afternoon. On cold days it may not take place until the afternoon.

The damselfly nymph emerges by swimming to shore. It swims slowly just below the surface of the water and stops periodically to rest. At the shore, the nymph climbs out of the water along a reed or weed and crawls out of its external skeleton. After its wings dry, it flies away. A good indication of a damselfly emergence is birds in the reeds feeding on the newly hatched damsels.

Casting technique.

- The appropriate fly is your size 12 golden Damselfly nymph.
- Use a floating line with a standard 9 foot 4X leader plus 3 feet of 4X tippet to create a 12-foot leader. Alternatively, use an Intermediate sinking line with a standard 9 foot 4X leader.
- In order to imitate the migration toward shore, anchor your boat in the weeds and cast out over the drop-off into deeper water. If the lake structure permits, one can stand on shore and cast into the deeper water.
- The objective is to move the pattern in a manner that suggests their swim which is a slow, wiggling motion close to the surface. Pull toward the weeds with the fly just under the surface. First try a slow retrieve with about 12-inch pulls. Pause every three or four pulls for up to 30 seconds. If, after awhile this retrieve does not work, change to a retrieve of continuous two-inch pulls as fast as you can. In either case, retrieve up to the leader.
- Strikes can come at any time, but are most apt to occur during the pauses.

Trolling technique. Use the same technique and equipment as in the early season. If trolling, go as close as possible to the shore and keep the fly near the surface.

How to Fish Mayfly Patterns During a Hatch

As stated earlier, only one species of mayfly is of major importance to the lake angler–the *Callibaetis*. Like all mayflies, the *Callibaetis* has a complex life cycle.

Only two stages are of importance to the beginning lake angler–the nymphal stage and when the nymph hatches on the water surface as a "dun". The preferred habitat of *Callibaetis* nymphs is among dense vegetation and they are found commonly on shoals no deeper than 20 feet and more often no deeper than 10 feet. When the nymph matures, it swims to the surface to hatch.

The mayfly hatch. The mayfly hatch occurs between mid-May and mid-June with the timing regulated by water temperature and daily weather patterns. The daily emergence is usually from 10 a.m. to 3 p.m. and is stronger if the sky is overcast, if there is a light breeze or if there is a light rain shower. The location of a mayfly hatch is determined by observing duns on the water, by the "bulges" as the trout takes a nymph just below the surface or by the "splashy" rises as a trout takes a dun off the surface. This hatch can provide exciting and productive action as trout often feed very actively on duns.

Anchor the boat upwind of the hatch activity in order to be able to cast easily into the feeding zone.

If you see mayflies in the air but not on the water, look upwind to find the hatch area. During a hatch trout may feed either on the nymphs as they ascend toward the surface or on the duns as they float on the surface. You should be prepared to fish both ways.

Casting technique for fishing the ascent
- The appropriate fly is your size 12 Pheasant Tail Nymph. You might also try your size 10 Halfback.
- Use an Intermediate line with the standard 9 foot 4X leader.
- Cast into the feeding zone and let the fly sink close to the bottom before beginning the retrieve.
- The objective is to imitate the nymph's movement as it swims to the surface on about a 20-degree angle. First try a very slow retrieve pausing periodically to let the fly sink. If, after a while this does not work, shift to a retrieve of quick pulls of about three inches pausing for a second or two

between pulls.

• Takes can be very aggressive, so be prepared.

Casting technique for fishing on the surface. Once the mayfly nymph is near the surface, the actual emergence of the dun takes place very quickly. Newly hatched duns do not move or swim around on the surface. Instead they sail along in the wind until their wings dry and then they fly away. Thus the movement to imitate when fishing the surface is a wind drift.

• The appropriate fly is your size 14 gray Adams.

• Use a floating line with the standard 9 foot 4X leader plus 3 feet of 4X tippet to create a 12-foot leader.

• Cast across at about a 45-degree angle to the wind and let the wind drift the line and leader. If there is no strike by the time the fly is downwind, retrieve with short, slow pulls with pauses of about 15 seconds. If there are rises within casting distance, cast to the centre of the ring, let the fly rest for a moment or two and then retrieve as above.

• A mayfly hatch allows for an opportunity to cast to specific fish rather than blind or random casting. Often you can see individual fish moving rapidly through the hatch area. Watch the rise forms to determine the direction the trout is moving. Cast in advance of this path to put your fly in front of the specific fish. The trout move quickly from one insect to the next so be prepared for a vicious strike.

Tips

• Dry flies need to be treated before they are used so that they maintain their buoyancy. For small or sparsely hackled dry flies, such as the Adams, use a spray floatant. For large or less delicate dry flies such as a Humpy use a paste type floatant. If after you have caught several fish, your fly no longer floats, change flies–this a another reason why you should buy more than one fly per pattern. Let the first one dry before using it again.

• Sometimes pulling the dry fly under the water surface and retrieving it with quick, short pulls can trigger a strike. Pulling dry flies under the surface and letting them bob to the surface can also trigger a strike.

Trolling technique. Trolling a fly through the hatch area during a mayfly hatch can be very productive.

- The appropriate fly is your size 12 Pheasant Tail Nymph. You might also try your size 10 Halfback.
- Use an Intermediate line with the standard 9 foot 4X leader.
- Troll into the feeding zone, stop your movement, let the fly sink close to the bottom, and then resume trolling slowly. The objective is imitate the ascent of the nymph.
- Because the duns only drift along the surface rather than moving under their own power, we do not recommend trolling adult mayfly patterns. However, as a troller you can put an Adams or Humpy on your floating line, move into the hatch area, stop your boat or tube and let the wind drift the fly through the feeding area.

How to Fish Caddis Patterns During a Hatch

The caddisfly or "sedge" progresses through the three stages of larva, pupa and adult. For the beginning angler, the pupa and adult stages are most important.

The caddis hatch. Caddis larvae live in depths of 20 feet or less amid dense weed growth. When fully developed, the pupa leaves the larval case and swims to the surface in a long ascending angle. It may swim just under the surface for some distance. During emergence, trout often key on the pupa, ignoring adults on the surface, especially if there is bright sunlight, the surface water temperature is high or if the surface is rough. Fully emerged adults pop to the surface and will either rest there or scamper around until their wings dry.

Seasonally, the emergence occurs from the middle of June well into July depending on elevation. Daily, the emergence is generally midday; however, some species emerge in the evening or at night.

Often the take of a caddis on the surface by a trout will be vicious, which is what makes a caddis hatch so exciting for the angler. The location of a caddis hatch is determined by observing the adults scampering on the surface, birds taking insects off the surface and by the rise form. Trout take the adult caddis with a splashy rise or even come up out of the water to come down on the insect. Anchor the boat upwind of the activity in order to be able to cast into the feeding zone.

Casting technique for fishing the ascent. To catch trout when they are feeding on caddis pupae as they rise to the surface to hatch, you should retrieve the fly to suggest the

swimming of the pupa. It swims to the surface in a long
ascending angle and, before emerging, swims just under the
surface.

- The appropriate fly is your size 10 green Carey. Also try your
  size 10 Halfback.
- Use an Intermediate line with the standard 9 foot 4X leader
  or a floating line with a standard 9 foot 4X leader plus 3 feet
  of 4X tippet to create a 12 foot leader.
- Cast into the feeding zone and use the count-down method to
  fish the entire depth because trout start feeding when pupae
  start swimming off the bottom and follow the pupae upward
  as they swim toward the surface.
- Retrieve with pulls of about six inches interspersed with a
  few shorter erratic pulls. If after a while there is no action,
  change the retrieve to a series of short, sharp pulls followed
  by a slow 18-inch pull and then a pause.

Tip

- Vary your retrieves. The emerging caddisfly
  pupa does not swim at a constant speed. At
  times the best retrieve is very slow.

Casting technique for fishing on the surface. The adult
caddis pops to the surface and, before flying away, spends a few
minutes resting and skittering around on the surface. The
objective is to suggest this movement.

- The appropriate fly is your size 8 adult caddisfly.
- Use a floating line with the standard 9 foot 4X leader plus 3
  feet of 4X tippet to create a 12 foot leader.
- Cast toward the adults on the surface. Look for a trout
  following a feeding pattern. If you locate one, cast to where
  you anticipate the next rise to be. In any event, take the slack
  out of the line immediately.
- Let the fly rest on the surface for a bit and then retrieve with
  quick pulls of about three inches. Throw in a 15-second
  pause at irregular intervals and then return to the quick pulls.
  If, after a while, there is no action, let the wind drift the fly
  and occasionally give the line a short twitch.

┌─ **Tips** ─────────────────────────────────

- One can also use a floating line with a pupa pattern when the pupae are swimming just under the surface.
- If circumstances permit, carry two rods in the boat–one with an intermediate line to fish the ascent and the other with a floating line to fish the surface.
- Fish often feed on pupae before the adults appear on the surface. As soon as you see an adult caddis, fish your caddis pupa pattern–the green Carey. When the fish are feeding on adults, fish on the surface with your adult pattern. After the surface feeding is over, go back to your pupa pattern, because trout continue to look for pupae even after the hatch is over.
- This is the one hatch where an anchored boat or tube is not recommended. You want to be as mobile as possible in order to pursue an actively feeding fish.

└──

Trolling technique. When trolling during a caddis hatch, use the same equipment described in the casting section.

Move your boat or tube in a manner that would duplicate the movement recommended for the retrieve of a cast fly. Note that during this hatch you can be effective trolling a dry fly. Allow your fly to trail behind you as you search for feeding fish. Troll slow enough so that the fly remains on the surface, but just fast enough to create a small wake behind the fly.

What to Fish in Prime Time When There Are No Hatches

It is not every day that hatches or emergences occur as we feel they should; however, we can rely on shrimp or leeches as a stand-by–either by casting or trolling.

Shrimp. If the fish are on the shoal, use an Intermediate line with a standard 9 foot 4X leader. If the trout are not on the shoal, then probe the drop-off area with a Type II sinking line and the standard leader. Remember to keep your retrieves erratic.

Leeches. If you are not successful with your shrimp

pattern, try a leech pattern. Fish with the same lines as for shrimp and in the same areas. Remember, your retrieve should replicate the undulating swimming motion of the leech

How to Fish the Imitative Patterns During the Summer Doldrums

Summer doldrums occur when the water warms and the fish seek cooler, deeper water with more oxygen and become virtually dormant. In this period one returns to shrimp, leech and dragonfly patterns and has these alternatives as to where to fish these patterns: deeper water, higher lakes, or at night.

Deeper Water

One alternative is to fish deeper water with sinking lines. In these circumstances very fast sinking lines are required. Use the most rapidly sinking line you own–preferably a Type III. When casting, position your boat or tube at the drop-off and cast toward the deep water. Use the count-down method to allow time for your pattern to get to the maximum depth and then begin your retrieve. If trolling, use the fastest sinking line you have. The foods available to the fish at this depth include shrimp, dragonflies and leeches.

High Lakes

Another alternative during the summer doldrums is to go to high altitude lakes (5,000 feet or higher) where the water is still cool. These lakes are typically lily pad lakes with dark water. The vegetation and the water colour result in less sunlight penetration which contributes to cooler water temperature. High lakes, because of their short season, are usually populated with smaller fish which can provide action when the lower elevation lakes are not producing. Fish the shrimp, leech and dragonfly patterns in the same manner as discussed in "prime time when there are no hatches". Trout love to hide in the shade and cover created by the lily pads. You can be successful by casting toward and beside the lily pads. Try your dry fly close to the lily pads–Walter may be lurking there. If trolling, fish in the same manner as in lower elevation lakes, but try trolling close to lily pads.

After Dark

Fishing in the evenings or after dark can be productive because, as the light fades, fish will move from the deeper water to forage in the shallower water of the shoals. Shrimp, leech and dragonfly patterns work well after dark, fished on either an Intermediate or floating line with the standard 9 foot 4X leader. In these low light conditions, use rapid retrieves in order to get the trout's attention. In addition, many caddis hatches occur at night; therefore, always have caddis patterns with you when fishing at night. When fishing after dark ensure that you have a good flashlight so you can see to tie on flies and find your way back to where you entered the lake. If you want to troll after dark, use your leech pattern and troll close to the shore.

How to Fish the Imitative Patterns During the Late Season

Late season is the period after the water cools and the doldrums end until freeze-up. The best fishing often occurs during this period and one returns to early season patterns. Late fall is a good time to catch large fish. As each frost cools the water, the larger fish seem to realize that freeze-up is approaching and they begin to forage in the shallows. Some of the best fishing occurs very close to shore. The weeds of summer have died. As a result, the trout's food sources have less protection and the weeds no longer inhibit the trout's movement. In addition, the birds that prey on trout have migrated to their winter range and are no longer a threat. Watch for trout rolling and splashing as they feed in the shallows. Leech, damselfly and shrimp patterns fished on either a floating or Intermediate line with the standard 9 foot 4X leader often produce the best results.

Closing Comments

Several times in this chapter we have recommended adding three feet of 4X tippet material to the standard nine-foot 4X leader to create a 12-foot leader when fishing a nymph on a floating line. In these cases, leader length is critical. All too often an angler next to my boat is not catching fish while my clients are. They will invariably ask what we are using, only to discover that they are using the same fly. My first question to them is always "how long is your leader" (knowing the answer will typically be seven feet). Given the same fly, our success stems from using the longer 12-foot leader. Use of this longer leader has been proven to be more effective when fishing wet flies on a floating line because it permits the fly to stay at the appropriate depth during the retrieve. Longer leaders also create less disturbance because the fly lands on the water further from the flyline. Leaders are a critical key to success! When your casting skills are well developed, we recommend that on a floating line you use at least a 12-foot leader at all times. **– Gord**

Chapter 7

Fishing the Chironomid Hatch

7. FISHING THE CHIRONOMID HATCH

The chironomid hatch is the longest and strongest of all the hatches. Chironomids are available to trout virtually all season. Since beginning anglers go fishing when they can, which may not be often, a book on how to begin flyfishing ought to stress techniques that are effective throughout the season. As well, beginning anglers often see others catching fish when they are not and as a result have a sense of frustration. Often those who are catching fish are fishing chironomids. Also beginners often regard a lack of knowledge about chironomid fishing as the biggest obstacle to their transition from beginner to skilled angler. For these reasons we have decided to include this chapter where we describe the "indicator" and "count-down" methods of fishing chironomid patterns.

Our Advice – Fish the Pupal Stage

The chironomid progresses through the three cycles of larva, pupa and adult. Chironomid larvae are bottom dwellers and are usually found in water less than 25 feet deep. They prefer alkaline waters and mud bottoms. When fully developed, pupae rise to the surface and hatch as adults. It is the pupal stage that is most important for the beginning angler.

Chironomid pupae do not swim to the surface, instead the movement is an ascent assisted by gas trapped beneath the pupal skin. During the ascent, the pupa maintains a constant undulating motion that keeps its head up and its tail down. Often it takes some time for the pupa to wriggle through the surface film. The transformation of the pupa to an adult at the surface generally takes less than two minutes.

Seasonally, the chironomid hatch begins when the water warms to about 50 degrees F. and continues until about August. There is also a fall hatch in September. On a daily basis the hatch begins about 9 a.m. When the water surface is calm, the emerging pupa can hang in the water surface for a long time, making it a ready food source for trout. When the water surface is broken by wind, the emergence occurs quickly and, after penetrating the surface film, the pupa will emerge as an adult. After its wings dry, it will fly away. In order to help you identify chironomids, we suggest you review the description in Chapter 2.

Trout feed on the chironomid in all its stages; however, it is our judgement that, for the beginning angler, it is most helpful to concentrate on the most important stage–the pupal phase–and to limit one's first attempts to a single depth–15 feet or less.

Enlarge Your Fly Box

In order to fish chironomids, you must expand your fly box to include chironomid pupa patterns. Refer to the colour photograph at the centre of the book and buy pupa patterns in three colours–black, green and brown–each in size 14. This size matches the average size of the chironomid pupa. At a later date you may want to add these same colours in size 12 and size 16.

Prerequisites for All Chironomid Techniques

Successful chironomid fishing requires that you:
- Find the area of the lake where the hatch is occurring.
- Determine the depth of the water in the hatch area.
- Anchor the boat or tube.
- Catch an emerging pupa or adult.

Locating the Hatch

The location of a chironomid hatch is determined by looking for swallows diving and taking insects off the surface. These insects are almost always chironomids. Go to this area and look for emerging pupae. If you only find shucks–those empty casings with white gill tufts–continue to search for emerging pupae by going upwind. On the surface of the water, you will see the adults crawling out of their pupal shucks.

Chironomid Shuck

Determining the Depth of the Water

The easiest way to determine the approximate depth is to mark your anchor line in five-foot intervals. A more accurate way is to make a sounder consisting of a thin line attached to a two-ounce lead sinker with knots in the line at five-foot intervals. If the depth is greater than 15 feet–move the boat. Stay within the hatch area and find a depth of 15 feet or less. Appropriate chironomid technique varies depending on water depth and, in our judgement, limiting oneself to water no deeper than 15 feet will accelerate learning. This depth is the easiest to fish and is highly productive.

Anchoring

While one should always use two anchors on a boat, it is imperative that two anchors be used when fishing chironomids because the imitation of the slow ascent can be destroyed by a quick sideways movement of the fly caused by a shift in the position of the boat. With a tube, only one anchor is practical and the angler may have to compensate for shifts in position by moving the rod tip.

Catching a Chironomid

Once the boat or tube is anchored in position, catch a chironomid–either a pupa or an adult. The purpose of catching a chironomid is to be able to match the hatch as to colour and size. The best way to capture a chironomid is to use a small aquarium net. You can lengthen the handle by taping the net to a dowel. The adult will be a size smaller than the pupa and lighter in colour.

The 'Indicator' or 'Bobber' Technique

When my clients call a corkie strike indicator a "bobber", I gently remind them the politically correct term is "strike indicator". If they look puzzled, I explain that you can purchase a bobber from Wal-Mart at a cost of 25 cents but for a strike indicator you must go to a "fly shop" and pay four dollars. – **Gord**

The first step in learning chironomid fishing is to master the "indicator" or "bobber" technique. The objective of this technique is to present a fly at a given depth, starting one foot off the bottom.

The role of the indicator is two-fold–to keep the fly just off the bottom and to signal strikes. For this technique:

- Use a floating line with a 15-foot 4X leader or the standard nine-foot 4X leader plus six feet of 4X tippet. A long leader is necessary for this technique in the water depth we recommend.
- Put an adjustable indicator on the leader. There are a number

of indicator systems available commercially. We suggest that you avoid the "stick-on" indicators, as they do not stand up to casting. We use either a corkie or a short length of yarn as an indicator. **These systems are illustrated at the end of this chapter.**

- Tie the appropriate fly pattern onto the tippet. Choose a fly that matches the colour of the body of the insects coming off. If uncertain, start with black, then brown and finally green. If the fly is unweighted, put a small split shot 12 inches above the fly (optional).
- Determine the depth of the water as accurately as you can.
- Adjust the indicator so that its position above the fly is equal to the water depth, minus one foot.
- Cast at a right angle to the wind. The cast need not be a long cast and this is just as well as it is difficult to make a long cast with an indicator.
- Let the wind straighten out the line and, as it does, the fly will sink toward the bottom.
- Do not retrieve the line; instead, just pull in enough line to keep a tight line between the rod and the indicator.

The indicator's first function, that of a float, will cause the fly to skim along just off the bottom. If the line is reasonably tight, the beginning angler should concentrate on the indicator's second function, that of signalling a strike.

The take of an ascending pupa by a trout can be very soft and often goes unnoticed by the beginning angler. The take is detected by watching for the "dip" or backward movement of the indicator. The angler's response to this soft take should be to "clamp" and gently lift the rod to the mid-position. A quick lift may pull the fly away from the mouth of the fish.

The point in starting with an indicator is to teach the beginning angler the importance of keeping a tight line in order to detect the soft take and just how soft the take can be. The advantages of the indicator technique are that it trains the eye and enables the angler, by adjusting the position of the indicator, to fish at various depths. One disadvantage is that it does not train the angler to detect soft takes by their feel. In addition, it creates a lag between the detection by sight and the reaction of setting the hook. This is undesirable because a slow reaction time can permit the trout to spit out the hook. These disadvantages bring us the second technique–the "count-down" method.

The Count-down Method

The first objective of the count-down method is to get the fly just off the bottom. The second is to systematically explore the water column in order to determine the depth at which the fish are feeding. The application of the technique to chironomid fishing in water 15 feet deep is:

- Use a floating line with the same leader as in the indicator method—either a 15-foot 4X leader or the standard 4X leader plus 6 feet of 4X tippet.
- Cast at a right angle to the wind. Let the wind straighten out the line and, as it does, the fly will sink toward the bottom.
- Let the fly sink for about one minute. (It takes an unweighted size 14 chironomid about one minute to sink 15 feet in calm water.) At first, do not guess at this interval but actually time it.
- The retrieve should be steady and very slow. Use tiny pulls—one-half inch or less. Retrieve until the butt of the leader is within about 10 feet of the rod tip. With this technique, fish often strike when the fly begins its ascent close to the boat.
- If you do not hook the bottom, increase the sinking interval by 15 seconds.
- If you hook the bottom, decrease the sinking interval by 15 seconds.
- If after a few casts, you do not have a strike, decrease the sinking interval by 15 seconds and continue to fish closer to the surface until you find the feeding zone.

In addition to locating the bottom and the feeding zone, the big advantage of the count-down method is that it trains the beginning angler to detect soft takes by their feel, thus reducing the reaction time. A more mystical advantage is that eventually one comes to "sense" the take, which for some is the appeal of chironomid fishing.

Chironomid Tips

Brian Chan, an acknowledged authority on chironomid fishing, states that the most common errors made by beginners when learning to fish chironomids are:

- Using flies that are too big–start with size 14 and if no action, go to size 16.
- Not letting the fly sink long enough–actually time the count down, do not guess.
- Retrieving too fast–as a rule of thumb, the retrieve should take twice as long as the sink time. If in doubt, retrieve as slow as you can and then cut the speed in half.
- Not keeping a tight line–stretch your line and leader and hold the rod tip close to or in the water to reduce line sag.

Trolling Tip

- The troller is not precluded from fishing the chironomid hatch: however, the troller should not try to match the hatch by trolling a chironomid pattern. Instead, troll a leech pattern through the hatch area. Fish may be attracted by a chironomid hatch, but will often feed opportunistically on leeches.

Closing Comments

Training questions aside, both the indicator and the count-down techniques are very effective.

The indicator technique is effective in shallow water (10 feet or less) because it permits the angler to hold the fly at a constant depth. If trout are feeding in shallow water their feeding depth is known and the need is to keep the fly in this zone.

The count-down technique is versatile. It can be can be used in water deeper than 15 feet either by using a longer leader or by using an intermediate sinking line. Further, it can be used any time one wants to fish just off the bottom.

If circumstances permit, try using both techniques at the

same time. Use two rods and with one fish an indicator "dead"–without a retrieve–and with the other use the count-down method and fish it "live"–with a slow retrieve.

There is a good possibility of a "double"–fish on each rod at the same time. Be sure you have the dead rod secured or in the excitement you could lose it overboard.

I didn't start flyfishing until I was 40 years old. Having discovered the sport late, I was determined to learn fast. I took a course in fly tying and learned how to tie a beautiful size 14 black chironomid pupa–the same pattern we have recommended to you.

One early spring day a friend and I took our boats to a favourite lake and on arrival we were greeted by the news: "The chironomids are coming off."

It was the first chironomid hatch I had ever seen and I was excited. The fish were gorging on the emerging pupae and my fly was a perfect match. I thought I couldn't lose–but I did. I didn't catch a single fish. My buddy, not encumbered by having tied his own fly, was yarding them in on a flatfish and kept encouraging me with comments like "these fish have eaten so many of those things that they look like they have swallowed a golf ball–why don't you get rid of that thing and put on a flatfish?" I ignored him, convinced that his comments revealed only that he knew more about golf than fishing.

In retrospect, I was making two errors.

The first was an inappropriate retrieve. I had learned how to tie a good fly but I had not learned how to fish it. I didn't catch fish on a chironomid until I learned and applied the count-down method. Then, one happy day, it all came together–four four-pound fish in an hour! I was converted and now am a true believer.

My second error was the one pointed out by my buddy–the wrong fly.

Paradoxically, it was too perfect a match. Given the hundreds of chironomids coming off, my fly had about one chance in a thousand of being noticed. In retrospect I should have differentiated my fly from the hundreds of pupae by using the same pattern in a much larger size or by changing to an attractor such as a black Doc Spratley. Alternatively, I should have switched to something that preys on chironomids–either a damselfly nymph or a dragonfly nymph.

Unfortunately, I have never seen another hatch of this magnitude, so like a general fighting the last war, I can only fish this hatch in my dreams. **– Ken**

Serious chironomid fishing is a fairly recent development and new fly patterns and indicators are coming out all the time. It is a consistently productive method of fishing. Mastering the techniques presented will reward you with many happy hours of successful flyfishing for trout in small lakes.

Walter escapes the net

Strike Indicators

Installation of a Corkie Indicator

A "corkie" is a floating ball of plastic with a hole through the centre. It comes in various sizes and colours and is available where bait-fishing gear is sold. We recommend a size 12, which is about half an inch in diameter. Get two or three in a colour that is highly visible. We prefer those with two colours—orange and chartreuse.

Do not tie your fly onto your leader until after you have installed the corkie.

To install the corkie:

- Run the tag end of the leader through the corkie.

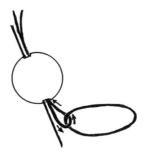

- Cut an 8-inch length of tippet material and insert it through the corkie beside the leader, through a rubber band, and back through the corkie.

- Pulling on both ends of the tippet material, pull the rubber band into and through the corkie.

continues next page **109**

Installation of a Corkie Indicator

continued from previous page

- Trim both ends of the rubber band.

To adjust the position of the corkie, just slide it along the leader until it is at the point where it will hold the fly at the desired depth. The corkie should stay at this position because the rubber band presses the leader against the inside of the corkie. If there is insufficient pressure to hold the corkie in position, use a thicker rubber band.

If this method seems too complicated, simply thread a corkie on the leader, slide it to the desired position and secure it by jamming the end of a round toothpick into the end closer to the rod. The desired depth of the fly can be adjusted by removing the toothpick, sliding the corkie along the leader and re-inserting the toothpick.

Installation of a Yarn Indicator Between Two Loops

If you are using a loop-to-loop method of connecting your leader to your floating line, an easy way to add a strike indicator is to insert a one and a half inch length of polypropylene yarn in the juncture of the loops.

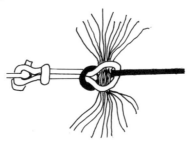

Polypropylene yarn floats; however, if it sinks squeeze the water out of it. You can coat the yarn with floatant, but be careful. Sometimes the floatant rubs off on the leader, causing it to float when you want it to sink. This strike indicator does not interfere with casting and, if necessary, it can be pulled through the guides on the rod; however, it is not adjustable.

Chapter 8

Improving Your Skills

8. IMPROVING YOUR SKILLS

This final chapter provides suggestions as how to increase your knowledge and improve your skills.

Learn More About Equipment

Chapter 3 provides an introduction to the vast array of equipment available for flyfishing. One way to increase your knowledge is to visit a local fly shop. Another is to get mail order catalogues. Three such catalogues are:

Cabela's
One Cable Drive
Sidney, Nebraska 69160-9555
(800+237-4444)

Kaufman's Streamborn Inc.
P.O. Box 23032
Portland, Oregon 97281-3032
(800+442-4359)

The Orvis Company, Inc.
Manchester, Vermont 05254
(800+548-9548)

Studying such catalogues will show you the characteristics and range of available equipment.

Learn More About Technique

One way to learn more about technique is to read books that are more advanced than this book. We recommend:

- Alfred G. Davey (ed.), *The Gilly* (Friesen Printers, 1985).

- Brian Chan, *Flyfishing Strategies for Stillwater* (Brian M. Chan, 1991).

- Ron Cordes and Randall Kaufman, *Lake Fishing with a Fly* (Frank Amato Publications, 1984).

- Jack Shaw, *Fly Fish the Trout Lakes with Jack Shaw* (Heritage House Publishing Co., 1998).

- Jack Shaw, *Tying Flies for Trophy Trout* (Heritage House Publishing Co., 1992).

Another way is to watch videos. We recommend:

- Brian Chan and Gordon Honey, *Flyfishing Strategies for Stillwater*, Volumes I and II (Stillwater Publications, 1995).

We also recommend for your education and enjoyment articles in flyfishing magazines, such as *American Angler*, *BC Outdoors*, *Flyfishing* and *Flyfisherman*.

Learn More About Tubing

Much of the emphasis in this book has been on casting from a boat. To learn more about techniques unique to fishing from a tube, we recommend:

- Robert Alley, *Advanced Lake Fly Fishing, The Skillful Tuber* (Frank Amato Publications, 1991).

- Marv Taylor, *Float-tubes, Fly Rods and other Essays* (Caxton Printers, 1997).

Learn More About Casting

As we said in Chapter 5, do not try to teach yourself to cast by reading a book. If you try, you will probably develop bad habits. We recommend you start by looking at a video such as Doug Swisher's *Basic Flycasting* produced by 3M's Leisure Time Products, get an understanding of what you have to learn and then get hands-on instruction. Lessons are often provided as part of an adult education program or by a local flyfishing club. Start by asking at a local fly shop. Once you have had hands-on instruction, go back to the video and start practicing.

Tip
- Often videos can be rented from fly shops or libraries.

Learn More About Insects

The sections by Brian Chan in *The Gilly* are an excellent next step to learning more about insects. We also recommend Jim Schollmeyer's *Hatch Guide to Lakes* (Frank Amato Publications, 1995).

Learn to Tie Flies

There are several reasons why a serious angler should learn to tie flies.

One is that if you tie your own flies you can make those that are not readily available over the counter.

Another is that it is satisfying to catch fish on a fly that you have tied yourself–especially if it is also your own original design.

Finally, flies you have tied yourself are apt to last longer than those you buy across the counter because you will have taken the extra time required to tie in extra knots.

Again we recommend that you take lessons, which are generally available from the same sources as are casting lessons. After you have taken lessons, ask the instructor about books and videos. We recommend:

- Skip Morris, *Concise Handbook of Fly Tying* (Frank Amato Publications, 1996).

- Philip Rowley, *Trout's Preference: A Collection of Proven Stillwater Patterns* (Frank Amato Publications, 1999).

Search the Internet

There are a number of interesting web sites on all facets of the sport of flyfishing.

Try Gordon's site at **bcadventure.com/ghillie** or under "Lake Fishing: Tips & Techniques" at **bcadventure.com**.

Join a Club

The main reason you should join a club is that you will meet other anglers and, from them, increase your knowledge.

It is your best avenue to learning more about the topics listed above as well as to inside knowledge about local lakes.

Hire a Guide for a Day

Consider hiring a guide for an intensive one-day clinic.

Ask questions prior to booking. In British Columbia, guides are licensed by the Fisheries Branch and must carry liability insurance. Accordingly, your first two questions are: "Are you licensed?" and "Do you carry insurance?"

If these are answered in the affirmative, then go on to ask questions such as:

- Do you provide intensive instruction or do you concentrate solely on fishing?
- What equipment do you provide? (If boats, ask about size–a proper guide boat should at least 14 feet long. If float tubes, ask about brand and whether waders and flippers are provided.)
- What tackle do you provide? (Make it clear to the guide what you are looking for and be candid about the level of your abilities.)
- Is there any additional rental fee? (If so, find another guide.)
- Are flies provided within the daily fee? (If not, find another guide.)
- May I have a list of references to past clients? (If you have any concerns, contact these references directly.)

To get the most out of your one-day intensive clinic, prepare a list of questions in advance and be ready to take notes during the day. Take along a video or audio recorder if you have one.

Concluding Comments

If the following question was posed to us, "What is the key element in becoming a successful angler?" we would respond, as one voice, "Observation". If we can leave you with three little words, they would be **observe, observe, observe**.

Without observation, your days on the water will always be based on luck rather than skill. Observation is a teachable skill and you are the teacher.

Your observation should begin as you approach the lake–look for jumping or rolling fish, birds, and anglers who have arrived before you. As you prepare your gear, take time to watch the lake carefully.

Once on the lake, go for a cruise. We both stand while

running our boats–thanks to a telescoping motor handle extension. (Do this only if your boat is very stable and if you are wearing a PFD.) This gives us a great advantage in that, by standing, we can see more of what is happening on the lake.

After you have decided how to begin–trolling or casting–continue to observe.

All too often we see anglers stay in one spot all day when 200 yards down the shoal, fish are rolling and other anglers are catching fish. You may need to move only a few yards to have a better approach to the feeding fish. Be prepared and willing to move. We will move 10 to 15 times during a day!

If you have field glasses, keep them handy and scan the lake every half-hour or so watching for the key signs. When you spot activity, move to it without hesitation. Keep your bug net handy and check those adult chironomids frequently for colour and size. If there is no hatch where you are, then go in search of one.

As you become a keen observer, you will note a phenomenon that occurs on every lake when the fishing slows down. As you scan your fellow anglers, you will find them with their heads down looking at their fingers. No, they are not hanging their heads in shame–they are changing their flies or searching their fly boxes for the magic fly.

A Final Note

Earlier we quoted Phil Rowley's axiom–"Change your retrieve more often than you change your fly." We would add to that wise counsel our axiom–if you change your location more often than you change your fly, you are well on your way to becoming an observant and successful angler. Good luck, be careful and courteous out there.

Appendix A

Terms You May Hear Anglers Use

Backswimmer—a beetle which appears in the trout's diet in the spring and the fall. It is not discussed in this book because it is not a major food source and because it requires more advanced angling techniques. Similar to the waterboatman.

Bloodworm—chironomid larvae having blood-red haemoglobin.

Bomber—a very large chironomid.

Coming off—a phrase indicating a hatch. As in "The mays are coming off" or "Have you seen anything coming off?"

False cast—a cast parallel to the water to extend the amount of line in motion as distinct from a "presentation cast" which ends with the fly landing on the water.

Foul hooked—when a fish is not hooked in its mouth but in some other part of its body. Generally, this is caused when a fish, at the last moment, turns away from a fly but, for example, hits it with its tail.

Glassworm—a charoboras larva, a cousin of the chironomid, which are small, transparent and difficult to imitate. When trout key on glassworms, fishing is "off".

Insect—a small invertebrate with three clearly defined body regions—head, thorax, and abdomen—with only three pairs of legs and usually with wings.

Larva (pl. larvae)—the immature, wingless and often wormlike form in which certain insects hatch from the egg, and in which they may remain, with increases in size and other minor changes, until they assume the pupa stage.

Midge—another term for a chironomid.

Molt—the process whereby an insect sheds its outer layer and replaces it by growing a new, larger outer layer.

Metamorphosis—a term to describe the stages of an insect's life. When the process has four distinct stages—egg, larva, pupa and adult—it is called a "complete metamorphosis". When there but three stages—egg, nymph and adult—it is called an "incomplete metamorphosis".

Nymph—a term sometimes used by anglers to refer to any insect in an underwater form: more correctly, it refers to the pre-adult stage in insects with an incomplete metamorphosis.

Pupa (pl. pupae)—an intermediate form assumed by insects after the larval stage and maintained until the beginning of the adult stage.

Scud—the zoologically correct name for what most anglers call shrimp.

Sedge—the British term for the caddisfly.

Shuck—a general term for the casings insects leave behind when they emerge or hatch.

Spooled—when a large fish takes out all your flyline and all your backing. As in "Walter spooled me."

Strike—this has two meanings—one is the hard take by a trout of a fly. The other is the action of an angler to set the hook after a trout has taken a fly.

Summer kill—when trout die in the summer due to lack of oxygen, usually caused by the increase in water temperature plus extensive blue-green blooms of algae.

Take—another term for strike.

Thermocline—the water layer which separates the warm upper layer from the more dense, colder layer (the metalimnion) which has little oxygen. For this reason fish are seldom found below the thermocline which is usually at about 25 feet and has a temperature of about 55 degrees F.

Turnover—the roiling of a lake in the spring just after ice-off when the cold layer which was next to the ice-layer sinks. Fishing is off until the water settles. As in "the lake is turning over."

Tag end—the end of a leader or tippet that is used in tying a knot. The other end which is not used is the "long end."

Waterboatman—a beetle which appears in the trout's diet in the spring and the fall. It is not discussed in this book because it is not a major food source and because it requires more advanced angling techniques. Similar to the Backswimmer.

Wind knots—a popular term for the knots in a leader caused by casting errors, not by the wind.

Winter kill—when trout die in the winter due to lack of oxygen, usually caused by the ice layer which prevents oxygenation of the lake plus the consumption of oxygen by plant life.

Knots

Tips on Tying Knots

- When first practicing tying a knot, do not use monofilament. Instead use string or cord that is thick enough so that the loops are easy to see. Using two contrasting colours will help. The string or cord should be stiff enough so that the loops do not sag. Try something like venetian blind cord or butcher's string.
- After you shift to practicing with monofilament, use long lengths. Once the mechanics of tying the knot with monofilament are learned, use shorter lengths. Our instructions show excess lengths for purposes of illustration.
- The key to strong knots is to avoid friction. Friction when tightening monofilament generates heat, which weakens it. Reduce friction by moistening the knot with saliva and by tightening it slowly.
- Master tying a tippet to a leader and a hook to a tippet before you go out on the water—especially if you are going in a tube.

How to Tie a Duncan Loop

A Insert the tag end of the tippet through the eye of the hook and along under the long end. This creates Loop 1 which holds the hook. Leave a very long tag beyond the eye–at least 7 inches.

B Create Loop 2 with the tag end.

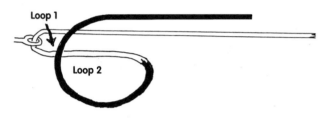

C Make five wraps over the long end and through Loop 2. With the thumb and forefinger of the right hand, pinch the tag end against the long end. Pull the lower part of Loop 1 toward the eye of the hook with the left hand to take the slack out of Loop 2 and to tighten the knot.

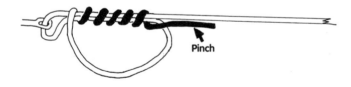

D Hold the knot between the thumb and forefinger of the left hand and pull on the tag end to tighten the knot. When the knot forms, slide it toward the hook eye until it is snug against the hook eye. Pull the knot tight and trim the tag end.

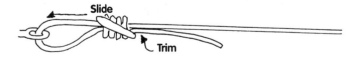

How to Hold the Knot
when Tying a Duncan Loop

- Make Loop 1 by wrapping the tag end around the last two fingers of the left hand and up to the forefinger to be held by the thumb.
- Make Loop 2 by continuing with the tag end to make a loose loop around the first two fingers of the left hand and hold it under the thumb.
- Make five wraps of the tag end around the long end and the top of Loop 2.

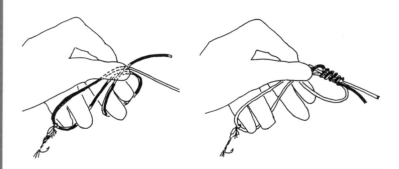

- Insert all the fingers of your left hand inside Loop 1 and, by expanding your fingers, tighten Loop 2.

How to Tie a Nail Knot

There are tools available which make it easy to tie a nail knot; however, we present a true "nail knot" in that a nail is used to form the channel through which to thread the tag end of the leader through the wraps. To tie a nail knot:

- Overlap the butt end of the leader and end of the fly line about six inches.
- Pinch with the thumb and forefinger of the left hand about three inches from the end of the line.
- Put a 2-inch nail along the line and pinch the head of the nail, the line and the leader.

- Wrap the tag end of the leader around itself, the line and the nail five times.
- Poke the tag end under the wraps, along the nail, and out the other end.
- Pull on the tag end to take out some slack.

- Shift the knot to between the thumb and forefinger of the right hand.
- Pull out the nail with the left hand.

continues next page

Nail Knot
(continued from previous page)

- Shift the knot back to the left hand.
- Take out the slack by pulling on the leader with the right hand until it is snug.
- Adjust the position of the knot if necessary.
- Moisten the knot and tighten slowly pulling on both the tag end and the long end.
- Tie it tight by holding the tag end in a pliers and pulling on the long end.
- Trim the ends.

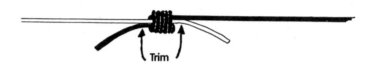

How to Tie a Perfection Loop

Trim

A   Hold the long end of the leader in your left and the tag end in your right. Make a loop by rolling the tag **BEHIND** the long end. After this loop is made the tag end ought to be about 4 inches long when learning the knot.

B   **HOLD** this loop, and all other loops, between your index finger and your thumb.

C   Wrap the tag end **AROUND** the first loop to create Loop 2. Hold with your thumb.

D   Wrap the tag end **BETWEEN** loops 1 and 2. Hold with your thumb.

E   **PULL** the top of Loop 2 **THROUGH** the top of Loop 1. Loop 2 will become the end loop.

F   **TIGHTEN** slowly, adjusting the end loop to the desired size–about three eighths of an inch.

G   **TRIM** the tag end.

┌─ **Tip** ──────────────────────
│ • Try inserting a wooden pencil in the end loop
│   and tightening the knot against it. This results
│   in a perfect perfection loop.
└────────────────────────────────

How to Tie a Triple Surgeon's Knot

The triple surgeon's knot is an overhand knot with three wraps. Many anglers use a double surgeon's knot–two wraps–however, tests show that a triple surgeon's knot is much stronger. To tie the triple surgeon's knot:

- Cut the desired length of monofilament from your spool of tippet material.
- Overlap the leader and the tippet material by about 6 inches.
- Grasp the leader and pinch the end of the tippet between the thumb and forefinger of the left hand.

Leader

Tippet Material

- Form a loop and pinch it between the thumb and forefinger.

Pinch

- Wrap both the tag end of the leader and the entire tippet through the loop three times.

- Moisten the knot and slowly draw it tight. Trim the tag ends.

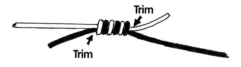

Trim

Trim

We Endorse These Manufacturers

FISHING LOG

Date	Time	Lake	Surface Water Temperature	Fish Species	Weight	Length	Fly	Weather Conditions	Other Notes

FISHING LOG

Date	Time	Lake	Surface Water Temperature	Fish Species	Weight	Length	Fly	Weather Conditions	Other Notes

FISHING LOG

Date	Time	Lake	Surface Water Temperature	Fish Species	Weight	Length	Fly	Weather Conditions	Other Notes

FISHING LOG

Date	Time	Lake	Surface Water Temperature	Fish Species	Weight	Length	Fly	Weather Conditions	Other Notes